HAVING HOPE
IN A
WORLD
WITHOUT HOPE

DANNY TICE

HAVING HOPE
IN A
WORLD
WITHOUT HOPE

ISBN: 978-1-949565-18-8

DEDICATION
This book is dedicated to my dad Roland Tice who constantly inspires me to live with integrity and to always extend grace to others..

CONTENTS

FOREWORD:

I have known Danny and Karen Tice since the late 1990s when I came to be their guest preacher. As a minister of encouragement, I was overwhelmed by their welcoming spirit and positive attitude. They exhibited to me a genuine faith, a fun faith if you will, in Christ Jesus. There was life in their fellowship. The lobby was full of positive attitudes and there was genuine evidence of healthy relationships. Even the countenance on the saint's faces was uplifting — full of Hope, Faith, and Love.

As the service was beginning, I truly enjoyed the welcoming of the visitors; it was so personal, so positive. Then to my amazement, they gave every first-time guest a freshly baked loaf of bread. I had smelled it coming into the church, but thought it was something for a luncheon after the service; I was blown away. I was so drawn by the sweet aroma that I took one myself. After church, they even let me have a second one! I love bread, especially fresh, homemade bread! Now that was special and unique, just like Danny and Karen and just like their church leadership. From that day forward they have extended grace to me and it has been my pleasure to speak for their fellowship several times. Through the years it's been a joy to keep up with Danny and the church through all the avenues of MEDIA.

Danny has been the Lead Pastor at Bay Shore for thirty-plus years. With Karen by his side, they have been the *Aquila and Priscilla* to Delaware and beyond. They've been successful because through it all, they have been relational leaders — positive servants and bold proclaimers of the truth in Christ Jesus. They understand the importance of encouraging one another now that His day is drawing near. (Hebrews 10:25)

Like Danny, I've had great parents that have passed on to me not only truth, but the spirit of truth. They gave me clarity for life's challenges with their own visible positive witness. I believe Danny probably *caught* this hope from his dad (a pastor for many, many years) instead of simply being *taught* this hope. Our loved ones project their legacy into our lives and generationally beyond. This *blessed hope* is essential in living in what often seems like a hopeless world. (Revelation 14:13)

You will enjoy this relevant and authentic book on Hope from a fellow soldier of the Cross — one who has been in the trenches and has learned the reality of Hope through relationships, attitudes, and biblical realities that make this book pertinent, enjoyable, and beneficial.

And just like my first visit to Bay Shore over two decades ago, Danny is still delivering the fresh and faithful bread of life, hot from God's oven, and filled with the aroma of Hope on every page! So, get yourself a cup of coffee and start reading; feed on every word and be encouraged.

Dennis Swanberg
America's Minister of Encouragement

HOPE IN A WORLD WITHOUT HOPE

Pastor Danny Tice is an especially gifted man who has and continues to play a pivotal role in my life. That being said, I confess that it is hard for me to be completely objective as I read the words he has penned. So, if you are looking for a completely objective critical analysis of this book you will not get it here! What you will get is a statement from someone who has known Pastor Danny for over 50 years. I have seen him in good times and bad. I have watched him live and lead day after day, season after season, decade after decade. I have had the privilege of observing him live out the principles and practices he shares in *"Having Hope in a World Without Hope"*. So when he says "this will help you" I read to get the wisdom being shared, the insight to be gained and the help that I can assimilate into my life and impart into the lives of others. *"Having Hope in a World without Hope"* is a timely book, filled with insights and encouragement that will be a benefit to "you"! Danny communicates in a comfortable manner that is easily understood and assimilated into life. I am thankful for the insights, wisdom and encouragement shared in *"Having Hope in a World Without Hope"*. I believe this work, born of love for Jesus and people, will accomplish the goal of helping people live better, more purposeful, hope-filled lives. Read it, enjoy it, live it…you will be glad you did…I sure am!

Sammy Fish, Church Planter, School Administrator and Life Long Friend

Long before there was a Covid-19 pandemic, there existed a global pandemic of hopelessness as evidenced by all the self-medicating taking place in our culture. Sadly, we've now lost significant portions of several generations to alcohol, drug, and sexual addiction. Among those who have not succumbed to addiction, there are many more who trudge along through life, just going through the motions, without hope for a better future. Pastor Danny Tice offers a very special kind of Hope available to all who would look to the source of enduring hope, Jesus Christ. He is an engaging writer who is both witty and wise in showing clearly how to discover the God kind of life changing hope. In this book, Pastor Danny offers insights that can only be gained after four decades of faithful service to Jesus and His Church. He is a kind and caring pastor who has walked with many folks through the darkest periods of their lives and given them hope through Jesus Christ. You will find hope inside the covers of this wonderful book.

Michael Bailey is an entrepreneurial business leader, church planter and mentor to pastors

"Pastor Danny Tice in his book; "*Having Hope in a World Without Hope*", captures the ingredient that helps us move from a life of mediocrity and even pain, to a place of vibrancy and hope. He draws from valuable lessons he learned from his father to the significance of having quality relationships, character building values, having hope when having hope is hard, breaking unhealthy habits and more. This book is immersed with life-given scriptures, Biblical wisdom and Christ centeredness. It paves the way to facing tomorrow with renewed courage rather than hopelessness and despair. *Having Hope in a World Without Hope,* is a prescription for the weary traveler that is looking to God for fresh Manna. This book will lift your spirits and give you a roadmap for attainable life of success and increased faith."

Fred Antonelli, Ph.D., former senior pastor, author, licensed mental health therapist and president of Elim Bible Institute and College in Lima, NY.

"The book, *Hope in a World Without Hope,* by Pastor Danny, encourages me to think and act in a more mindful manner and to focus on what is to come. Pastor Danny has shared personal moments and insightful hope during a most challenging time. Pastor Danny connects with his readers and inspires individuals to apply Biblical principles to their daily lives."

Ruth Briggs King, 37th District Representative of the State of Delaware

Danny Tice writes from a well-lived life in Christian leadership, with all of the normal joys and sorrows, ups and downs, victories and tragedies. He writes with a familiar friend by his side. That friend is Hope. While "Having Hope" grows from one person's journey, with numerous stories and examples to anchor the reader in reality, the book is more than anecdotal observations. In the final chapter, Tice writes, "...it will be difficult to have hope if you do not believe that history is heading somewhere." Tice builds his case from Scripture's timeless truth and a single eternal principle: When we align ourselves with God's purposes, we will never be without hope and it will always be our steadfast friend too.

Doug Gehman, President, Globe International, Pensacola, Florida

1

HOPE: ADJUSTING YOUR ATTITUDE

"The greatest discovery of any generation is that a human can alter his life by altering his attitude." William James

My dad is my hero. He is the one that led me to Jesus when I was twelve years old. He has demonstrated to me over the years what it means to be a follower of Jesus. One of the things I know about my dad is that he is consistent. His faith is steady, and he has a positive attitude about life. My dad has pastored the same church for almost fifty years. I have watched my dad weather many storms: church splits, criticism from parishioners, and all the things that go a long with being a pastor. He has taught me how to walk in love and forgiveness. My dad is an excellent preacher, but his greatest skill is loving people who have not been nice to him. Of all the qualities my dad has, this is the one that I want to learn from him. He is better at forgiving others than I am, but as his student, I am gradually learning to forgive more effectually.

My dad is not perfect, but he is an optimist when it comes to people. He believes that no one is hopeless, and everyone deserves forgiveness and second chances. My dad believes there is hope for everyone, so he is quick to extend grace. My dad has taught me that grace promotes hope; judgement promote despair. During my dad's tenure as pastor at the church he leads, Christ Evangelistic Church, there was one man in particular who was especially difficult to deal with. Life serves up some people to all of us that are just difficult. This man was the epitome of difficult. He accused my dad of some things that were not true, but my dad weathered these accusations with the love of Jesus. Like anyone, my dad was tempted to get bitter and angry. Instead he chose to forgive.

My dad is an avid bowler, and at the time he bowled in several leagues. My dad graciously invited this man to be on his bowling team so he could spend time with him and deepen their relationship. I marveled at his kindness. His love and patience melted the man's heart and the relationship was restored. Some would call my dad naive to bring an adversary so close to his bosom, but my dad believes it's better to be naive than paranoid! In a world where there is love and forgiveness. there is always hope.

My Dad Dealing with Grief

The hardest thing my dad has ever gone through was learning to have a positive attitude toward life after my mom died. She suffered from dementia for years, but my dad faithfully loved her and served her and took care of her. I was deeply impacted as

I saw him take care of her every day. Love is more than words, and my dad demonstrated this to me every day. When she died on July 21, 2019, it was the darkest day of his life. He was enshrouded by grief. They had been married for sixty-two years and shared every aspect of life together; he was lost without her. However, my dad, being a man of prayer and the Word, gradually got back on his feet and continued to preach and serve people.

During this difficult time, my dad had some serious health issues of his own. He recovered from his own physical challenges and kept moving forward. I take my dad out to dinner weekly, and when I pick him up, he always has a smile on his face. When I say "always", I mean "always." My dad's smile and positive attitude is not fake or disingenuous; it is solid and real. I never find him feeling sorry for himself. I certainly realize that he is sad and lonely sometimes, but my dad, like all of us, is human. However, he is tenacious; he's a picture of strength and steadiness. Life has been hard for him, but he has never lost his smile, his confidence, and his desire to live life to the fullest. He often tells me, "Life is short. You better take time to enjoy it."

This book is about how to live life to the fullest. It is about how to have hope when things seem hopeless. Living life to the fullest doesn't require our lives to be perfect. This is a good thing because no one's life is perfect. When you are going through a tough time, one of the things to tell yourself is, "I am not the only one." That is true. Whatever you are facing, there are scores of people on this planet who are dealing with almost exactly what you are dealing with. We are all in this together.

No One's Life is Perfect

When we start a new year, we all wonder if this is going to be a good year or a bad year. Our thinking goes like this: if a lot of good things happen to me this year, I will have a great year, but if a lot of bad things happen, I will have a horrible year. In other words, we tend to wait for the outcome before we decide if it was a pleasant or poor experience. I call this "condition-based living." If the conditions are good, I will be happy; if they are not good, I will be unhappy. If you are waiting to see what will happen before you decide whether you will have a good day, a good month, or a good year, then your attitude has placed you in a powerless position. Hopeless people feel powerless because they assign their mental and emotional state to something that is outside their control. I don't know about you, but the last thing I want to be is powerless! Unfortunately, a feeling of powerlessness over an extended period can lead to depression and despair. Such a view means we have determined to be a victim to whatever happens to us. Are you ready for the truth?

Every day, every month, and every year has a mixture of good things and bad things. There is no such thing as a perfect year, perfect month, perfect day, or perfect life. No one has a life where everything that happens is good. If that description of life sounds like your life, then welcome to the human race. When we look to outside circumstances to assess if we are having a good or bad year, a good month or bad month, or a good day or bad day, then we are assuming a powerless position. Think of it as adopting a *victim's mentality*, feeling powerless, waiting for and allowing circumstances to dictate the quality of our life. The problem with being a victim is we place other people or outside circumstances in charge of the quality of our life. However, the liberating truth is no one has to be a victim, regardless of what has happened to them or around them; my dad's smile is proof of this.

TAKE CHARGE OF YOUR DAY

The book of Psalms teaches us to have a positive proactive attitude before we start each day. Psalms 118:24 says,
This is the day the Lord has made; let us rejoice in it and be glad.

The Psalmist in essence says, this day belongs to God and I am going to rejoice in it. The contents of the day are never the issue, but the focus of our attitude is what matters. Psalms 118:24 certainly sounds like we have a choice in how we approach each day. Here are two principles that are essential for choosing to have a great life:

Having a great life is not based on what happens around me, but the attitude that I have in me.

You can never control everything around you, but you can always control the attitude inside you.

Successful people have concluded they will not obsess about what they can't control but will focus on what they can control. If you are a person that likes control, I have both good news and bad news for you. The bad news is you cannot control all the things that happen around you. Conversely, the good news is you can always control the attitude inside you. When you start to be overwhelmed because there are things in your life you cannot control, you must accept the fact that you cannot always control all things that happen in your personal environment.

THE POWER OF ACCEPTANCE

Acceptance is one of the most powerful attitudes a person can possess. Always remember acceptance is powerful! Denial strips people of power while acceptance gives them power. However, when you feel things are out of control, tell yourself, "I *can* control what is happening inside me right now. I don't have to be a slave and a victim to things that are occurring around me." We must recognize the difference between "out there", which is my environment, and "in here", which is my attitude. If you possess an "in here" philosophy of life you are going to have a good life. People with an "in here" way of thinking discover that their life can be good even when there are bad things happening around them.

CAMELLIA LIZARDS IN FLORIDA

When Karen and I first got married, we moved to Pensacola, Florida, where we attended Bible College. We lived in a house that had a beautiful yard with two giant pecan trees in the backyard. There were gorgeous azalea bushes around the house that majestically bloomed each spring. One of the things that I distinctly remember about living in this house was that the yard had an abundance of camellia lizards that lived in the yard. Sometimes the lizards would get in the house and we would frantically chase them around and try to catch them in a jar in order to relocate them outside. What is unique about camellia lizards is that they possess the capacity to change colors. If they are situated on a brown stick, they will turn brown. If they are on a bright green leaf, they will turn green. These lizards become the color of their immediate environment. Unfortunately, a lot of people are like camellia lizards. If things are good, they are happy; if things are bad, they are sad. These lizards are reflectors —they merely reflect their surroundings. We are not supposed to be reflectors of our environment; we are to transcend it with a positive attitude.

THE DIFFERENCE BETWEEN REJOICING AND BEING THANKFUL

Paul says in the book of Philippians that we are to rejoice in the Lord. Specifically, he states: "Rejoice in the Lord always. I will say it again: Rejoice!" (Philippians 4:4) Did you know that there is a fundamental difference between being thankful and rejoicing? When we are thankful or grateful, we have something specific in mind. Rejoicing is different. When we rejoice, we are acknowledging that the Lord is in charge and sovereign over everything happening in our lives. Thankfulness works like this: we are thankful that we got the promotion, or that we got a new pickup truck. We are thankful that a certain girl said yes to go out on a date, or that our children got into the right school. Thankfulness is a good thing; it is very specific and is connected to something tangibly good that is happening or has happened. The Bible tells us we are supposed to be thankful.(Psalms100:1-5, 1 Thessalonians 5:18, Philippians 4:6). Thankfulness is directly connected to an answered prayer or something specifically positive that happened to us.

OUR FIRST NEW HOUSE

I remember when I got the call that Karen and I had been approved to get our first house. We were living in a mobile home next door to the church we pastored in Delaware. Karen and the kids were not home when the bank called to say our loan was approved. I will never forget receiving the good news that we were going to get a new house. We had always lived in subpar rentals or mobile homes during our college days and our early years of ministry. When I got the call from the bank for our loan approval, I was ecstatic; we were getting a house! I had a basketball goal in the backyard of the mobile home we lived in beside the church, so I grabbed my basketball and went outside, grinning from ear to ear. I spent the next forty-five minutes shooting hoops and feeling thankful that the Lord had helped us to buy our first home. The modest home was wonderful, and we lived in it for fifteen years while raising our sons. Thankfulness is like that. There is something specific that is good that has happened to you, and it fills your heart with that warm feeling that makes you grateful.

REJOICING IS CONNECTED TO GOD'S SOVEREIGNTY

Rejoicing is different than thankfulness. Rejoicing isn't connected to a few good things that have happened in your life. Paul didn't say rejoice about something specific; he said, "Rejoice in the Lord." We rejoice not because something good happened, but because the Lord is sovereign in our lives. We rejoice "in the Lord" because He knows what He is doing when it comes to our life; He has authority over our destiny. We rejoice because God is guiding and directing our lives. The Bible says, "The steps of good man are ordered by the Lord." (Psalms 37:23 KJV). Remember, thankfulness is connected to a positive thing or things God has done for us, while rejoicing is connected to God being the ultimate ruler in our lives. You and I can celebrate because God is in charge of the details that relate to you and me. I love this quote by Charles Spurgeon:

"God is too good to be unkind and He is too wise to be mistaken. And when we cannot trace His hand, we must trust His heart."

I love this quote because it has proven to be true in my life. The fact is we don't always know which way is up or down, but if we know that God is in charge, we can have peace. God is ultimately guiding our lives so we can be tranquil even when things are difficult. Remember God is wise, God is kind, and He has never made a mistake! That means God doesn't make mistakes when it comes to your life and mine, and He holds you and me in His hands. (John 10:28)

REJOICING IS WEATHERPROOF

When Paul admonished the folks at Philippi to "rejoice in the Lord", he was in prison. Ironically Paul's most positive letter, the book of Philippians, was written from jail. One would expect any letter coming from jail to be laced with doom and gloom, but Paul's letter from jail was filled with hope and encouragement. Paul was living what he preached. The word "joy" or "rejoicing" is used sixteen times in this little letter from Paul. We tend to think that rejoicing is conditional. If the conditions are right, then we rejoice. We can rejoice in the Lord because our futures are in the hands of the Lord. Rejoicing is rooted in God's overarching plan for our lives, not in current circumstances.

A BIG STORM

Many years ago, I went through a very dark time in my life. Most of us have had some dark seasons in our lives; a loved one dies, a spouse has an accident, or a family member has cancer. There are trials in life and then there are TRIALS! My dark time involved some very challenging issues at the church where I had led for over thirty years. The issue was significant enough that it impacted the staff, the congregation, and the surrounding community. I wondered if the church would survive, and I wondered if I would survive! Then one morning as I was reading my Bible devotions, a scripture spoke clearly to me. I was reading through the book of Genesis 6-9 about Noah going through the famous flood. At the end of the story about Noah surviving the flood, a brief genealogy was given. Genesis 9:28 says, "After the flood *Noah lived 350 years.*" As I read that phrase that morning in my devotions, I heard the Lord speak to me. He said to me, "You are going through a great storm, but after the storm, like Noah, you will have a long and fruitful ministry." That word from the Lord was not audible, but it was the voice of God's Spirit whispering in my heart. It was exactly what I needed to hear. The thing I realized at that moment was God was with me; He *did* have a plan; I was going to be ok, and my family and church would be ok as well. I could rejoice in the Lord because He was in charge. I could rejoice even in the most difficult time in my life because the Lord was ultimately guiding my life.

When you are going through a dark time, it is easy to hear all the wrong voices. During my dark time at the church, I was criticized by many people that didn't really know the details of the situation. When you are surrounded by a sea of criticism, God's voice, through the Bible, is your life raft. A word from the Lord can give you confidence and hope; a word from the Lord can break the depression in your soul. That word from the Lord that day proved to be true. Many years later, I can say I went through a great flood and I survived. Not only did I survive, but ultimately the ministry of the church grew and was blessed. Maybe your great flood is different than mine. Maybe you have experienced a painful divorce or the death of a loved one or friend. Maybe you have a physical illness. or perhaps you have gone through bankruptcy. It doesn't matter what the source of your flood is, God has a future for you. Then after your great flood, your future can be bright and full of promise.

Discussion Questions:

1. Has there been a time in your life when there were obviously parallel things that were positive and negative going on in your life at the same time?

2. How can you apply the two statements below to a particular circumstance that you are currently going through? Having a great life is not based on what happens around me, but by the

attitude that I have in me. You can never control everything around you, but you can always control the attitude inside you.

3. What spiritual truth did Paul understand that helped him to rejoice when he was in jail?
4. How was his positive attitude an inspiration to the church at Philippi?
5. What is the primary difference between being thankful and rejoicing in the Lord?
6. How can Noah's longevity after the great flood encourage us when we are going through a horrific trial in life?

2

HOPE: POSITIVE RELATIONSHIPS

"The ability to deal with people is as purchasable a commodity as sugar or coffee and I will pay more for that ability than for any other under the sun.:
John D. Rockefeller

Red Pollard

One of my favorite films is the movie, *Sea Biscuit,* about the undersized thoroughbred racehorse that inspired millions of Americans during the Great Depression. In my view, **Sea Biscuit** is one the most inspiring movies I have ever seen. I love the movie, and I can't confirm nor deny that I may have cried a few times at the conclusion of the film. My favorite character in the movie is Red Pollard played by Tobey Maguire. Pollard was the jockey of Sea Biscuit. Pollard was psychologically damaged because his Canadian parents gave him to a horse trainer to raise him during the Great Depression because they could not afford to take care of him.

Consequently, Pollard has underlying anger issues that surface time and time again throughout the movie. In order to earn extra money because he is on his own, Pollard engages in illegal boxing matches. He rarely wins, but boxing seems to be a way for him to work out the simmering anger that is inside him. In a memorable scene in the movie, Pollard is at a horse training center surrounded by three of four men he has picked a fight with. He keeps them at bay as he yells and swings a bridle at them. That scene seems to be a metaphor of his life,: Pollard against the entire world! Throughout the movie his anger perpetually alienates others around him. It is at this point in the movie that the horse trainer, Tom Smith, played by Chris Cooper, notices him and hires him as Sea Biscuit's jockey. Through Pollard's relationship with Smith and Sea Biscuit's owner, Charles Howard, played by Jeff Bridges, Pollard finally finds a family and is loved and accepted. Although there are several times when Pollard's behavior warrants dismal as the jockey, Charles Howard loves and accepts him, and refuses to dismiss him. Through this love and acceptance, Pollard's character begins to change and his anger dissipates. As the anger diminishes, all of Pollard's relationships drastically improve. Ironically, it is love and acceptance from others than makes Pollard a loving and accepting person. Love and acceptance changed Pollard's heart, and as a result, he was able to love and accept others.

THE QUALITY OF YOUR LIFE

It is impossible to have a great life without great relationships. There is a correlation between the quality of our relationships and the quality of our lives. The formula for success in life looks like this:

Positive Relationships = A Positive Life

If the quality of our relationships is high, then the quality of our life will be high; if the quality of our relationships is low, then the quality of our life will be low. In order to improve our lives, we must improve our relationships. It is encouraging to know that if we adjust this single area in our lives, then we can vastly improve the quality of our lives. Therefore, we need to place a great deal of effort on getting better at relating to others. The 26th President of the United States, Teddy Roosevelt, once said, *"The most important single ingredient in the formula of success is knowing how to get along with people"*.

Roosevelt elevated relational intelligence to "the most important" element to anyone's success in this world. Improving our relationships is something we all need to pay diligent attention to if we are going to have a happy and successful life.

DIFFICULT PEOPLE

Getting along with others is sometimes, maybe even often, complicated and difficult. Some relationships are more challenging than others. Frankly, some people are very challenging and require a lot of grace to get along with. Everyone has certain people that try their patience and drain them emotionally. When Winston Churchill was Prime Minster of England, 1940-1945, he had a political nemesis that constantly harassed him. The name of Churchill's personal thorn in the side was Nancy Astor. Astor was a prominent member of Parliament (1819-1845) and had regular interaction with Churchill. Churchill and Astor were arch political enemies and could barely agree on anything. She despised Churchill and he despised her. She once said to the Prime-Minister, *"Sir, if you were my husband, I'd poison your tea."* Churchill responded, *"Madame, if you were my wife, I'd drink it!"* Astor and Churchill couldn't stand each other. Churchill once quipped, "I want nothing to do with that woman!" The truth is we all have people that are difficult to get along with. It may be a sibling, a coworker, a neighbor, an ex-spouse, a daughter-in-law, a son-in-law, or even one of your grown children. Getting along with others is not easy. In fact, having positive relationships is one of the most difficult challenges anyone will face. It is not always easy to live in harmony with others. So, if you have a difficult relationship that is troubling you, you are not alone. Challenging relationships are a universal experience, but getting better at getting along with others will help you have the life you have always dreamed of having. A series of failed relationships can make us feel hopeless. However, if you have a failed relationship you may not be responsible for the status of that relationship. It takes the cooperation of two parties to have a positive relationship.

Initiating the Restoration Process

Whenever there is a failed relationship, the Lord may deal with us to seek to repair it. Ultimately, as we will shortly see, the restoration of the relationship is not only our responsibility, but we may be nudged by the Lord to reach out to someone that we have a broken relationship with. Twelve-Step programs call this "making amends" with people we have hurt and wounded. In a broken relationship, we have either been wounded or have wounded someone else, sometimes inadvertently. In other words, we probably share some measure of blame for why the relationship is off track. It most likely is partially our fault and partially their fault, but we are only responsible for our part. The key to making amends is that you make the first move. Too often, we are waiting for the other person to make the first move, but God is conversely tapping us on the shoulder to start the process. Jesus said if you are at the altar making a sacrifice and recall you have someone that has an issue with you, leave your gift and go seek reconciliation. Matthew writes in Matthew 5:23-24 23 *"Therefore, if you are offering your gift at the altar and there remember that your brother or sister has something against you, 24 leave your gift there in front of the altar. First go and be reconciled to them; then come and offer your gift."*

I have many times written a letter of apology or made a phone call to someone to ask their forgiveness for some part I played in the demise of our relationship. Recently I wrote a letter to a family member that I had a strained relationship with. It was regarding a weight I was carrying every day, so I wrote a note owning my stuff in the failed relationship. A few days later I received a warm response back with a desire to patch up the relationship. I was thrilled! In my letter I didn't pressure them to repent of their stuff; I just took care of my stuff. Then in response, they owned their stuff. This isn't always the outcome, but it can be when we repent of our mistakes and sins toward another person.

Pick Up Your Dirty Socks

When Karen and I first were married, we lived in a little one-bedroom cottage. I was young and not a very tidy or responsible husband. One of my great faults was leaving my dirty socks on the floor. This frustrated Karen so she confided in a little old lady that lived a few cottages down. Her name was Miss Annie. Several times a week Miss Annie would walk down to our cottage and rap on the door. When I went to the door, Miss Annie would simply ask me, "Are you picking up your dirty socks?" Through these brief interactions, I found out that in order to have a good marriage I needed to pick up my dirty socks. I gradually improved at this and marital bliss returned. Life is about picking up your dirty socks; this is code for taking responsibility for your messes. The book of James says, "Confess your sins to one another...that you might be healed." (James 5:16)

The Relationship Dance

The tricky thing about relationships is relationships are like dancing; it is a two-person enterprise. It takes two people to want a positive relationship to make that positive relationship a reality. The good news is you are only responsible for your part of the relationship. The bad news is if someone is uncooperative in getting along in a relationship, you are powerless to change them. Realizing you can't change other people is one of the most liberating ideas a person can embrace. You are only responsible for your attitude toward them. A very comforting scripture on relationships is found in the New Testament book of Romans. Paul said to the Christians at Rome,

"If it is possible, as far as it depends on you, live at peace with everyone." Romans 12:18

What a liberating verse! *If it is possible*—that means that sometimes you have done everything you can to have a positive relationship, but the other party is simply unresponsive and unwilling. A negative relationship does not mean that you have failed. It may mean that the other party is unwilling to do their part. Paul indicated, "...as far as depends on you." In other words, it takes two people to dance and you cannot control the actions or the attitude of another person. I tend to beat myself up when I'm in a broken relationship I can't fix. I want peace with everyone, but sometimes I just have to tell myself that I have exhausted everything in my power to make the relationship work. The ball is in their court; the rest depends on them. Sadly, some people prefer conflict over peace and harmony. Success in relationships always depends on both parties because it takes two willing people to have a good relationship.

DIRT MOUNDS AND TUNNELS

When I was young boy of about six-years-old, I made my first friend. His name was Henry. Ironically his last name was Henry as well. His middle name was Lee, so his full name was Henry Lee Henry. I recall a time we were playing on a big, black, dirt pile not far from my house. The hill was located at an abandoned construction site. Henry and I played on those dirt piles for hours, having dirt chunk fights (throwing clods of dirt at one another). After a while, we decided to make a tunnel through the top of one of the mounds. Digging tunnels on a dirt pile is an exhilarating experience which I highly recommend to everyone. Henry got on one side of the dirt pile and began to dig, and I was on the other side. We were digging with all our might as if we were constructing the Holland Tunnel. After a long time, we finally broke through. Our little arms were submerged up to our arm pits and our hands were touching in the middle of the tunnel. We pulled our hands out and could look straight through to the other side; it was a euphoric moment for two little mischievous boys. "Mission completed," we thought to ourselves.

When I think of that childhood memory of digging the tunnel with Henry, I think of relationships. Relationships are like digging a tunnel. Each person must deal with the dirt on their side of the relationship. When two people are both dealing with the dirt on their particular side, there can be breakthrough in any relationship. However, if one party is unwilling to deal with their dirt, the relationship cannot move forward. If you have tried to reconcile and heal a relationship, but the other party has not exerted any effort in restoring the relationship, you are not to blame! Quit beating yourself up and accept the fact that you cannot control what other people do. Conscientious people tend to carry false guilt over unresolved relationships when the other party isn't cooperating in the reconciliation process. When this happens, it's best to accept the reality that there is nothing else you can do. Be at peace and suspend all self-blame you may be directing to yourself. God gave us all the freedom and right to make our own life choices. Unfortunately, when those choices do not align with His, hardness of heart can enter, and resistance to reconciliation can prevail over unity. In these types of cases, accepting the other party's choice, whether right or wrong, is a way to liberate your soul from feeling guilty about an unresolved relationship. You may still be sad because the relationship is out of order and not working, so turn your sadness into prayer for that person, and ask the Lord to minister to them. We are called by God to pray for and bless our enemies (Matthew 5:44).

TRYING MATTERS TO GOD

Remember that God is pleased with you when you have tried to make a relationship work even if you have not succeeded. In the Old Testament, King David wanted to build a temple for the Lord. Yahweh told David that he was not the one to build the temple because he had been a man of war. (1 Chronicles 22:8, 28:3) Instead, his son Solomon would build the temple. However, the Lord told David even though he wouldn't build the temple, He (God) was pleased that David had a heart to do so. The author of the book of 1 Kings 8:17-18 writes:

17 "My father David had it in his heart to build a temple for the Name of the Lord, the God of Israel. 18 But the Lord said to my father David, 'You did well to have it in your heart to build a temple in my Name. NIV

Your desire for a positive relationship is pleasing to God even if the other party declines to participate in reaching that noble goal. Quit beating yourself up for the broken relationship you have sought to repair.

Now we turn to one of the most important components of positive relationships. That component is kindness. If we are going to have great relationships and live in a world of hope, we must become skilled at being kind to others.

BE KIND

One of the most important virtues in developing successful relationships is kindness. Being kind to other people greatly enhances the possibility that our relationships will succeed and thrive as we step into a world of hope. There is a myriad of scriptures that highlight the importance of kindness. One scripture says that we should clothe ourselves with kindness each day. In other words, just as we get dressed every day, we should put kindness on as we start our day. Paul writes,

> *"Therefore, as God's chosen people, holy and dearly loved, clothe yourselves with compassion, kindness, humility, gentleness and patience."* *(Colossians 3:12)*

People that walk with Jesus should exude kindness toward others. Kindness is one of the fruits of the Spirit. When a person is filled and saturated with the power of the Holy Spirit, one of the virtues that emerges is kindness.

I grew up in a charismatic/Pentecostal church. My dad was the pastor, and we talked a great deal in our church about being full of the Holy Spirit. Although my theology has changed some over the years, I have positive memories of my Pentecostal/charismatic heritage. In that religious tradition, we emphasized that being filled with the Spirit enabled a person to speak in tongues, prophesy, minister divine healing to the sick, and to be filled with boldness to witness to others about Jesus. All these things are good and positive, but unfortunately, they do not entail the entirety of the potential effect of the Spirit ruling our lives. The book of Galatians, however, gives an additional list of what it means to have the Spirit ruling in our lives. Paul said that the fruit of the Spirit is expressed in nine wonderful characteristics. These Spiritual virtues are traditionally called the fruits of the Spirit. When a person is adorned with the fruit of the Spirit, they have the character of Jesus; to have the fruit of the Spirit is to live and act like Jesus. One of those virtues of the fruit of the Spirit is kindness. Paul writes,

> *22 But the fruit of the Spirit is love, joy, peace, forbearance, kindness, goodness, faithfulness, 23 gentleness and self-control. Against such things there is no law. (Galatians 5:22-23)*

The fact that kindness is a fruit of the Spirit means that Holy Spirit must help us to be kind. As humans we can tend to be impatient, frustrated, and abrupt with others. Perhaps a good thing to do right now is to say, "Lord I want to be kind like Jesus, and I cannot achieve that without your supernatural help." When you ask the Lord for virtues that will make you more like Jesus, God is pleased with your request for kindness. He will then begin to endow you with a supernatural ability that transcends your natural abilities. 1 John says that if we ask anything that is in His will, He will give us what we ask of Him. (1 John 5:14) It is certainly God's will to make you more like Jesus, so you can be assured that a prayer to be kind like Jesus will be answered by your heavenly Father.

BEING KIND BENEFITS YOU

One of my favorite verses about kindness is found in the book off Proverbs. This verse reminds us that when you are kind to others, you help yourself. Notice what Solomon writes in Proverbs 11:17,

17 Those who are kind benefit themselves, but the cruel bring ruin on themselves.

Let those words sink in — "Those who are kind benefit themselves." When you are kind to others, you bless yourself. I frequently remind people in my church that you cannot help another person without helping yourself. There are great benefits that come to a person that is kind to others. If you want to enhance your life with joy, good things, and perpetual hope, then be kind and benevolent to others. The Hebrew word for "benefit" in Proverbs 11:17 is "gamal" and means to receive recompense or to be rewarded. Literally, "gamal" means to "deal out to." When you are kind to others, good things are dealt out to you. There are positive personal benefits when you are kind to others. We should be kind to others because it is the right thing to do, but we must not forget that when we are kind to others, we are being kind to ourselves. Our lives go much better when we are an emissary of love and kindness instead of anger and bitterness. There are many benefits that come back to you when you are kind, but if you are mean and cruel to others the opposite happens. When you are cruel and mean to others, you only hurt yourself. The second part of the Proverb 11:17 says, "but the cruel bring ruin on themselves." Being mean, angry, difficult, and harsh with others will come back to haunt you. Being unkind to another person is being unkind to yourself.

34

If you want to elevate the quality of your life, be proactively kind to others. In doing so, your life will receive great benefits. Conversely, this Proverb says that when you are unkind to others, you bring destruction on yourself instead of a blessing. I desire benefits, not destruction, and I am sure you do as well. So let's roll up our sleeves up and work on our kindness skills!

MEAN HAMAN

In the Old Testament book of Esther, we see that meanness and cruelty can destroy us. Haman was the assistant to Xerxes the Persian King. Haman was cruel, vindictive, and vengeful to a man named Mordecai. Mordecai was a Jew who was one of the main characters in the book of Esther. Mordecai had done Haman no harm; he simply refused to bow to him. As a Jew and a monotheist, Mordecai was not permitted to express worship to anyone but Yahweh. (Esther 3:2) This enraged Haman because he had a massive ego and wanted everyone's adoration. Haman devised a plan to persecute all the Jews because of his anger toward Mordecai. Haman deceived the King into signing into legislation a plan to exterminate all the Jews that lived in Persia. Haman, filled with bitterness toward Mordecai, had a gallows built in his backyard. His plan was to get permission from the King to lynch Mordecai on the gallows. Haman was cruel, mean, and the antithesis of kindness. In the end, the tables are turned, and Haman was hung on the gallows he had built for Mordecai. Haman's cruelty brought destruction on himself. The story of Haman confirms Proverbs 11:7, "the cruel bring ruin on themselves."

Always remember being kind to others is being kind to yourself; being mean to others is ultimately being mean to yourself. A mean, unkind, and vengeful man is a man that saws off the limb he is sitting on. Success in life is directly connected to being kind to others and avoiding being angry, cruel, and vengeful at others. We currently live in a world that is losing hope. Hope can be restored to the world with an army of people, armed with love and kindness.

How Do I Know What Kindness Looks Like?

There is a simple guideline for determining what kindness is. A famous Rabbi who was a contemporary of Jesus, was asked if he could summarize the entire law while standing on one foot. His name was Hillel. His response is memorable. To summarize the entire law while standing on one foot means that the summary must be succinct and quick. Hillel said,

"What is bad to you, don't do to someone else. Now go and learn." Rabbi Hillel

Hillel nailed it! To treat others the way you want to be treated is to understand what true kindness looks like. When you are dealing with someone in your life, project your face onto their face. See yourself in the person that is in front of you. Ask this ancient question, "How would you wish to be treated?" You certainly would like to be treated with mercy and patience, and you would want to be given the benefit of the doubt. Kindness is exporting to others what you wish others would export to you. This is the golden rule given to us by Jesus. Luke gives us this profound teaching from Jesus. Luke writes,

"Do to others as you would have them do to you." Luke 6:31

When we employ that guideline, "Do to others as you would have them do to you", defining kindness is simple. Kindness is merely a matter or painting your face on the person right in front of you. Finally, let's look at three people or groups you need to be kind to.

BE KIND TO YOURSELF

It is essential that you are kind to yourself. If you aren't kind to yourself, you cannot treat others kindly. You must love yourself before you can love others. If you hate yourself, you will hate others. If you are critical of yourself, you will be critical of others. If you are impatient with yourself, you will be impatient with others. Our relationship with others is really an overflow of our relationship with ourselves. Ironically, having successful relationships begins with having a good relationship with yourself. Scriptures are not ambivalent about our call to love ourselves. We are commanded to love ourselves! Jesus, Moses, Paul, and James, the brother of Jesus, repeat the great commandment to love your neighbor as you love yourself (Leviticus 19:19, Matthew 19:19, Mark 12:31, Mark 12:33, Luke 10:27, Romans 13:9-10, Galatians 5:14-15, James 2:8).

"And the second is like it: 'Love your neighbor as yourself.' All the Law and the Prophets hang on these two commandments." Matthew 22:39-40

How are we to love our neighbor? Like we love ourselves! This passage commands us to love **both** our neighbor and ourselves. It should be noted that God loves you extravagantly. (1 John 3:1) If you love something, you are willing to pay a great price to obtain that item. For example, if you see a piece of waterfront property that you love, you will likely be willing to pay top dollar for that property. If you find a car or truck that you really love, you may choose to pay a considerable amount to purchase that vehicle. Likewise, God sees your great worth, so He gave Jesus for your salvation. The scriptures say you are not your own; you have been bought with a price. (1 Corinthians 6:20) God paid the ultimate price for your redemption because His love was great toward you. Your great value is confirmed because God gave His best, Jesus, to redeem you. God thinks you are awesome, so you should think you are awesome as well.

BIOLOGY CLASS

When I was a college student at the University of Delaware working on my undergrad degree, I had to take a biology class. The class was very challenging and exam grades were coming in very low. In order to retain a scholarship, I needed a good grade in this class to keep my GPA up. I sat in the front row of the class, took copious notes, and even taped the class to listen to it a second and third time. The professor was brilliant; he would fill the chalk board with biological formulas and terms that had to be memorized to pass the class. I was never tempted to stand up and say, "Dr. Curtis, you don't know what you are talking about! I totally disagree with your scribblings on the chalk board! You are wrong about these formulas and terms!" I didn't do that because he had a PhD in Biology and I was taking Biology 101. Dr. Curtis knew what he was talking about so who was I to disagree with him? He was the expert on biology, and I was clearly not. When it comes to our worth, who are we to disagree with God? He loves us, so who are we to not love ourselves? The Lord knows everything about us and still loves us and considers us worthy of His divine affection. The New Testament says that "God has lavished his love on us." Precisely, 1 John 3:1 says:

> How great is the love the Father has lavished on us, that we should be called children of God! And that is what we are! The reason the world does not know us is that it did not know him.

God's love toward you is not conservative; it's radical. Lavish is not a term I use often but it is a great word. Notice this definition of *lavish* from dictionary.com, "to bestow something in generous or extravagant quantities on." God poured out His love on you in abundance. If that is the opinion of God toward you, how could you have such a low opinion of yourself? You are to love yourself because you can't really love others until you love yourself.

OUR FAILURE DOES NOT ERADICATE HIS LOVE

The number one reason people have such a low opinion of themselves is that they have trouble forgiving themselves for their sins and failures. We have all sinned and fallen short of God's glory. (Romans 3:23) So what are we to do when we sin? As followers of Jesus, 1 John 1:9 encourages us, "If

*we confess our sins, He is faithful and just to forgive us
of our sins and to cleanse us from all unrighteousness."*

This was my favorite verse as an adolescent. As a
Christian in high school, with so much temptation, I
was constantly claiming 1 John 1:9 when I sinned.
Because I am still in the process of being sanctified
and made more like Jesus, 1 John 1:9 is still an
important verse in my walk with Him.

One day I was reading 1 John 1:9 and noticed a
word I had overlooked for all the years I had been
reading that verse. It was the word *"we"*. Scholars
are convinced that John the Apostle, who laid his
head on the breast of Jesus at the Last Supper (John
13:23), was the author of the gospel of John and
also of 1 John. The writing style in the Greek is very
similar, therefore scholars conclude that the gospel
of John and that of 1 John must be written by the
same person. The day I noticed the word *"we"* as
I read 1 John 1:9, it occurred to me that John, the
beloved Apostle, included himself in the need for
daily cleansing and forgiveness. John did not say
"if you" confess your sin; he said if "we" confess
our sins. How encouraging that discovery was for
me that day. John said to his audience that all of
us, including himself, needed daily forgiveness by
the blood of Christ. Even apostles need to ask for
forgiveness for their sins because after all, we are all
part of the same human family.

A LEADER WHO SINNED

I once had a leader in our community come to
me for counseling. He had sinned in a dramatic way
and was feeling a great deal of shame. I met with
him for several sessions, but his sense of guilt and

shame was overwhelming. My efforts to point him to grace seemed to have little effect on him. One day as I was meeting with him, I asked him, "Do you know why you are persisting in your guilt and shame?" I continued, "It is pride!" He looked at me with shock at such a suggestion. I then said, "You think the Cross is good enough for everyone else to be forgiven, but you hold yourself to a higher standard than everyone else." His pride had convinced him he was special and should know better than to do what he did. When I confronted him with his pride, it broke that sense of shame he had been under. He saw that he needed to humble himself like every other human being, and gratefully receive the full forgiveness of Jesus. The Cross isn't the means of forgiveness for *some*, it is the means of forgiveness for *all* of us. He began that day to recover from his guilt and shame.

Christian counselor Henry Cloud says that he is not a fan of guilt because guilt has no meaningful value after we ask the Lord to forgive us and change our behavior. The bottom line is no one is above their need for the Cross. John said "if *we*" confess our sins. Even Apostles receive forgiveness just like the brand-new Christian receives forgiveness. No one ever outgrows the need for the Cross.

BE KIND TO PEOPLE THAT ARE DIFFERENT

Because we have received mercy and forgiveness from the Lord, we are set up to be kind to others, especially people that are different than we are. It is easy to be nice to people who are like us in thought and philosophy. However, we tend to struggle being kind to people who are different than we are.

My sons took me to a professional football game one December. My boys are Baltimore Ravens fans. I am a Green Bay Packer fan but support the Ravens as my back-up team when my main team is doing terrible. The game my sons took me to was on a Thursday in Baltimore. The Baltimore Ravens were playing the New York Jets. We walked to the stadium down the street and there were tailgate parties everywhere. The smell of burgers and brisket filled the air and was accompanied by the chanting and yelling of Ravens fans coming from every direction. The atmosphere was filled with excitement and energy as the Ravens were headed toward the playoffs. There were literally thousands of Ravens fans, all dressed in their Ravens paraphernalia, lining the streets around the stadium, and ready to see the Ravens crush the Jets. The Ravens fans were ecstatic, in full party mode. Lamar Jackson, the Ravens QB, had the Ravens in a winning streak and the fans were optimistic about the game that was about to start.

As we were walking toward the stadium, we noticed a couple of people that were New York Jets fans. They were wearing New York Jets Jerseys and beanies. The Ravens fans began to yell at them, taunt them, and hurl profanities at them. I had conflicting thoughts about these Jet fans. First, how brave and courageous to wear their team colors to a Ravens game. Second, how stupid to wear their team colors to a Ravens game! The fact is, we tend to be unkind to people that are different than us. We tend to reject and push away people that think differently, are a different race or ethnicity, or have a different philosophy than we have. We tend to reject and deny them kindness if they have different doctrinal beliefs, different political views, or different traditions than we have as well. Chuck Swindoll once included this little poem in one of his books:

"Only then I'll Fellowship With You"
Believe as I believe—no more, no less;
That I am right (and no one else) confess.
Feel as I feel, think only as I think;
Eat what I eat, and drink but what I drink.
Look as I look, do always as I do;

And then—and only then—I'll fellowship with you.

When we only cheer for and are kind to people that are just like us, then we are not very noteworthy. Anyone can be loving and kind to someone just like themselves. To love and to be nice to people that are just like us is natural, but we are called to transcend the natural and to live supernaturally.

CALLED TO ELEVATED LIVING

If we love and are kind to people that are just like us, that is no big deal. Jesus said in Luke 6:32-36:

32 "If you love those who love you, what credit is that to you? Even sinners love those who love them. 33 And if you do good to those who are good to you, what credit is that to you? Even sinners do that. 34 And if you lend to those from whom you expect repayment, what credit is that to you? Even sinners lend to sinners, expecting to be repaid in full. 35 But love your enemies, do good to them, and lend to them without expecting to get anything back. Then your reward will be great, and you will be children of the Most High, because he is kind to the ungrateful and wicked. 36 Be merciful, just as your Father is merciful."

Jesus said it is natural to love people that wear the same jersey as we wear. However, we are called to supernatural living, not just doing what is natural. Anyone can be nice to people that are just like they are. However, people that have the capacity to love and be kind to people that are radically different than they are live an elevated life.

Max Lucado tells a marvelous story in an article he wrote a number of years ago called "Rising Above Our Hurts." Lucado expounds on the unique relationship between Stephen Douglas and Abraham Lincoln. Lincoln and Douglas were of different political parties and had very different political views. Specifically, Lincoln and Douglas had big differences about the issue of slavery. Lincoln believed slavery should be limited to the territories to which it already existed. Douglas, on the other hand, believed in popular sovereignty. This was the doctrine that stressed that States should decide for themselves if slavery should be permitted in their region. In 1858, Lincoln and Douglas were running for the same Senate seat in the Illinois Legislature. Douglas was the incumbent Senator and Lincoln was seeking to unseat him. They agreed to have seven debates throughout different counties in Illinois. The Lincoln-Douglas debates became famous and were attended by thousands of people. Douglas won the Illinois election in 1858, but in 1860, Lincoln was elected the 16th President of the United States.

This was largely due to the fame Lincoln garnered during the debates.

On Inauguration Day, as Lincoln was about to give his inaugural speech, tailors, seamstresses, and well-wishers outfitted Lincoln with a beautiful custom-made suit, an overcoat, a large top hat, and even a cane with an ebony handle the size of large goose egg. Lincoln was unaccustomed to all this elaborate attire. When he was introduced, he walked up to the podium and people applauded and cheered. Lincoln was a bit nervous, not about his speech, but about what to do with his cane and his top hat. Lincoln stood there awkwardly for a moment, contemplating what to do with these items. He finally leaned the cane against the railing but was at a loss to know what he should do with his top hat. He thought about putting it on the top of the podium, but it would take up too much space. He then thought about putting it on the floor by the podium, but thought the floor was too dirty for such a fine hat. As he was awkwardly trying to figure out what to do, a familiar friend came up behind him and took Lincoln's hat and held it during his speech. That friend was Stephen Douglas. During their famous debates Lincoln and Douglas became friends even though they had very different political views. Although they disagreed with each other, they learned to be civil and kind to one another. Lincoln learned to admire and love Douglas and believed he could trust Douglas with his life. It was Douglas who escorted Mary Lincoln to one of the grand balls after the inaugural speech, and during Lincoln's finest hour, Douglas had been willing to kindly hold his friend's hat. Even though Douglas had also run for President in 1860 and lost to Lincoln, his support for his friend was undeniable. During the early years of Lincoln's administration, Douglas was Lincoln's greatest ally. Douglas traveled to southern states promoting Lincoln's policies, begging them to not secede from the Union. Worn out from his travels, Douglas died a few years after Lincoln's election. Upon his death, Lincoln openly wept at the death of his friend. Some historians speculate that Douglas would have been Lincoln's running mate in 1864 and therefore would have succeeded Lincoln when he was assassinated. Sadly, we will never know if that would have happened. However, what we do know is that two political opponents who disagreed about many things, learned to be kind to each other. They learned how to live an elevated life.

In America. people have become politically divided and have lost the art of civility. Even when we disagree with each other as Republicans, Democrats, and Independents, we need to learn from the story of Lincoln and Douglas by showing kindness to people who are different than we are. If we are going to create a beautiful world of hope, we need to develop the art of kindness in our culture.

BE KIND TO PEOPLE THAT ARE CLOSEST TO YOU

Sometimes we are kind to complete strangers, yet we are mean and terse to people in our own family. How many Christian families have yelled and fussed at each other on the way to church, only to walk in the door of the church to be sweet and nice to people that are non-family members. We give the best version of ourselves to strangers and the worst version of ourselves to our family. We should be kind to people that are closest to us. The Miami Dolphins most famous quarterback was perhaps Dan Marino. He was one of the NFL's greatest quarterbacks during the 1980s. Every Christmastime, Marino was the spokesmen for the Isotoner glove company. Isotoner gloves were not cheap; they were high quality gloves that made great Christmas presents. Each of the Marino commercials featured him buying gloves for his offensive front line. The big burly men that made up the Dolphin front line were responsible for blocking for Marino as he stood in the pocket looking for open receivers. Marino's tag line for his Isotoner glove commercial was, "Take care of the people that take care of you." I love that! When it comes to being kind, we should be most kind to the people that are closest to us. We should be nice to the people that take care of us. Taking care of the people that take care of you is one of the highest expressions of kindness. Of all the people on this planet, your spouse, your kids, and your family need to see the best version of you. Be kind to them.

Getting along with others is one of the great keys to success in life. If you want a great life, seek great relationships. Do your best to get along with others and you will find your best life.

Discussion Questions

1. Do you have some difficult people in your life that are challenging to get along with?
2. What are somethings you have learned that work in dealing with difficult people?
3. What are some things you have discovered do not work in dealing with difficult people?
4. Discuss some steps that you can go through to seek to be reconciled to people that you are estranged from.

5. Who does reconciliation ultimately depend upon?
6. How can developing a lifestyle of kindness enrich our lives?
7. What are the three groups of people that we need to be kind to?
8. Who can help us achieve kindness toward others — especially people that are different from us?
9. Why is a life of kindness a supernatural endeavor and not a natural endeavor?
10. Why is loving yourself essential in order to love others?

3

THE BIBLE AS YOUR ANCHOR FOR HOPE

"Take all that you can of this book upon reason, and the balance on faith, and you will live and die a happier man."
Abraham Lincoln

My High School Bible

I went to Seaford High School in Seaford, Delaware. SHS was not a Christian high school, and as a follower of Jesus, I was definitely in the minority there. I loved my time in high school and have many life-long friends from that season in my life. My best friend was Sammy Fisher. I had the privilege of leading Sammy to the Lord when we were freshmen. Sammy and I helped each other as we attempted to walk with the Lord in our worldly high school environment. We were just normal adolescents trying to follow Jesus but seeking approval of our peers in a world dominated by temptation. One of the things that I tried to do as a Christ follower in high school, was to take my

Bible to school every day. This encouraged daily opportunities to tell people about Jesus. Inevitably I was daily asked, "Why are you carrying a Bible to school?" That question always gave me a prime opportunity to tell people about Jesus.

A few years back, our high school class had its 40th class reunion. I was asked to lead a service remembering our classmates that were deceased. I stood in front of my classmates and was able to minister to them from the Bible. Some of the people facing me at the memorial service that day used to make fun of me for being a Christ-follower. Now many of them listened with rapt attention. Growing older can cause a person to reevaluate earlier shallow worldviews! After the memorial service, we toured our high school. Memories and nostalgic thoughts flooded our minds as we walked down the hallways we used traverse as adolescents.

As I was walking down the hall with two classmates, David Smith and David Keiser, they said to me, "Do you still have that green Bible you brought to school every day?" I responded, "Absolutely!" That green Bible is in my home office and every time I look at it, I remember how it sustained me through those challenging years.

The Bible has also played a major part in my life since then. One of the wisest things anyone can do is to read it every day. Reading the Bible everyday will constantly fuel hope in your heart. Before writing this chapter, I read the Bible in the morning. I felt peace and strength as I feasted on its pages. Reading the Bible is a daily habit for me, and it is a habit you should consider implementing in your life if you want to be a person of hope.

A SPIRITUAL GPS SYSTEM

Recently I drove to Philadelphia to visit a friend and congregant that had brain surgery in Jefferson Hospital. His name was Bob Obergefel. Bob and his wife, Brenda, are wonderful members of our congregation. Bob and Brenda sit in the second row to my right, and when I preach, they are like sponges as they take in the scriptures. When I left my home to visit Bob in Philadelphia, I turned on the GPS in my Tacoma pickup truck. It gave me the approximate time of arrival plus detailed instructions on how to get to Philadelphia, specifically to Jefferson Hospital. During the trip when I came to an exit I was supposed to take, the GPS would remind me ahead of time and give me specific instructions on where to turn. Philadelphia is a big metropolitan area, very different from my rural surroundings in southern Delaware. However, I had complete confidence in the GPS system. I arrived successfully in a little over two hours, and before I knew it, I was visiting with my friend Bob and his wife, Brenda.

The GPS system helped me because I was traveling to a place I was unfamiliar with. Life constantly takes us to unfamiliar places: we leave home and go to college, we get a new job, we transfer to a new city, we become parents, the kids grow up and move out, we retire, or we lose a spouse or a loved one. Life is perpetually changing and every change we experience produces some anxiety and uncertainty.

In order to deal with the changing landscapes of life, we need ongoing direction on how to navigate these new, unfamiliar places. Without a spiritual navigation system in our lives, we can quickly loose our hope and confidence. Nothing is more helpful than the Bible when it comes to dealing with changes in life. Ronald Reagan once said, "Within the covers of the Bible are the answers for all the problems men face." Reagan was right. The Bible is adequate to help us through each and every issue that we face in life. It may not always give us specific direction on who we should marry, or where we should buy our next home, but it will give us a foundation to make decisions that are in alignment with God's character and ways.

NEVER BEEN THIS WAY BEFORE

In the book of Joshua in the Old Testament, we see the story of succession. Joshua took over for Moses after Moses died. Succeeding Moses had to be a tough assignment. Moses was the man that led Israel through the Red Sea and was the bestselling author. Remember Moses' literary hit, "The Ten Commandments?" I imagine that Joshua had to feel a bit apprehensive about his new role and taking the position formerly held by someone like Moses. Basically, God was telling a high school freshmen basketball player to come off the bench and replace Michael Jordan! Joshua was walking into a space in life that he had never been in before. The Lord gave Joshua precise instruction about how to go about this transition, probably a transition that he was highly apprehensive about. Here is what it says in Joshua 3:1-4,

3 Early in the morning Joshua and all the Israelites set out from Shittim and went to the Jordan, where they camped before crossing over. 2 After three days the officers went

throughout the camp, 3 giving orders to the people: "When you see the ark of the covenant of the Lord your God, and the Levitical priests carrying it, you are to move out from your positions and follow it. 4 Then you will know which way to go, since you have never been this way before. But keep a distance of about two thousand cubits between you and the ark; do not go near it."

The key phrase in this passage is found in verse 4 that says, *"since you have never been this way before."* That is life in a nutshell. We constantly come to places that we have never been before. God's instruction to Joshua and the people he was leading was that they were to look at the ark of the covenant as they headed to their new and unfamiliar destination. Most people are familiar with the ark of the covenant from the famous movie *Indiana Jones and the Raiders of the Lost Ark* starring Harrison Ford. The ark of the covenant was a real thing and not just something made up by Hollywood.

The ark of the covenant was a wooden box covered with gold that contained the tablets of the Ten Commandments that Moses received on Mount Sinai. That means the inside of the box was God's divinely inspired word. When Joshua and the Israelites went to this new place, they were to keep their eyes on the ark that contained God's word. The lesson is clear: we need guidance when we go to new places in life. The place to find that guidance is God's word.

READ PROVERBS EVERY DAY

One of the ways I obtain guidance for the new phases of life is I read God's word every day. I find incredible comfort and strength in reading the scriptures regularly. One of the portions of scriptures I read over again and again is the book of Proverbs. Proverbs is a portion of scripture that Biblical scholars term "Wisdom Literature." Proverbs is filled with wisdom about everything we deal with in life. Proverbs covers such pertinent subjects as handling money, raising children, anger, sexual lust, relationships with friends, old age, and a host of other practical subjects we face in life. Proverbs is conveniently divided into thirty-one chapters which means there is a Proverb for each day of the month. I am in the habit of reading the Proverb that corresponds with the day of the month it is. So if it was April 8th, I would read Proverbs 8, or if it was May 2nd, then I would read Proverbs 2. I have learned so much from Proverbs. Some of the spiritual axioms found in this marvelous little book guide me in practical ways every day of my life. I have hope for each day because I receive practical wisdom regarding how to live my life in the midst of a crazy world.

READ SYSTEMATICALLY

The best way to read the Bible is to read it systematically. The Bible is not a fortune cookie that gives you a little prediction for each day. Don't just throw open your Bible and stick your finger on a verse and read it for guidance; read the Bible systematically, book by book, chapter by chapter, and verse by verse. My method of reading the scriptures is that I read two Old Testament chapters, one Proverb, and two New Testament chapters a day. It usually takes about twenty-five to thirty minutes. I read the OT and NT chapters in order, one book after another, book by book, chapter by chapter, and verse by verse. You don't read the Bible through and put it on the shelf like you do other books; you read it over and over again. Each time you read it through, you will see something new. Additionally, you should read it again and again because your life is constantly changing, and certain portions of the Bible have special applications to you during different seasons in your life.

CHECK: DONE READING THE BIBLE!

Each January our church gives out Bible reading programs to help inspire individuals to read the Bible regularly in the new year. We also point them to the YouVersion app that has a variety of Bible reading programs. I have a man in my congregation that is a very disciplined and structured person. This man took our Bible reading program and read through the whole Bible by the month of May. He proudly told us he had finished the Bible! We gently encouraged him that you never finish the Bible. We never finish reading the Bible until it is finished with us. The goal is not to read the Bible through once and say, "I have finished reading the Bible." The goal is to read the Bible time and time again until it is finished making us like Jesus. Of course, we are constantly growing in Christ and will not be totally like Him until He returns, or we go to heaven. (1 John 3:2)

A NEW KING'S FIRST ASSIGNMENT

When someone became a new king in Israel, the first thing he was to do was to make a personal copy of the Hebrew scriptures. It should be noted that there were no copying machines in ancient Israel, so the king's new copy of the scriptures had to be made completely by hand. Moses records these instructions for a new king in Deuteronomy 17:18-19:

> *18 When he takes the throne of his kingdom, he is to write for himself on a scroll a copy of this law, taken from that of the Levitical priests. 19 It is to be with him, and he is to read it all the days of his life so that he may learn to revere the Lord his God and follow carefully all the words of this law and these decrees. NIV*

Moses states, "He is to write it for himself." The new king was to have a personal relationship with God's word. This is important. You cannot have a secondary relationship with God by merely listening to sermons from your pastor. Although hearing God's message through your pastor is still vital for your walk, you need to have an intimate and personal relationship with God through His word each day. The new king had to sit at a desk and copy the Hebrew scriptures, word by word. Moses went on to say, "It is to be with him all the days of his life."

We need God's word with us when we are young, when we are middle-aged, and when we are old. God's word is something we always need. We never put the Bible on the shelf or in our office or in our desk drawer. We need to open it every day, 365 days a year. When we open it, we learn Who God is. We understand His ways and it helps us with our decisions. It will keep us, strengthen us, and make us people of hope. Someone once said that a Bible that is falling apart usually belongs to someone who isn't. The reason the Lord had the new king make his own copy of God's word was so that it would become an integral part of him.

COPY OVER AND OVER AGAIN

When I went to college, I figured out how to get A's and B's. I wasn't the smartest guy in class, but I discovered if I took good notes in every class and then recopied them later in the day, I would internalize and learn the material. I can't remember who told me to do this, but I remember the first semester I implemented this practice. I was amazed! I got great grades just by employing that little habit of copying my notes a second time. When you read the Bible repeatedly, this power book becomes a part of you. It changes how you think and how you look at the world so you can perpetually be a person of hope.

THE SWORD OF THE SPIRIT

Paul described the Bible as "the sword of the Spirit" in Ephesians. He writes:
Ephesians 6:17

"Take the helmet of salvation and the sword of the Spirit, which is the word of God." NIV

I think the metaphor of God's word being a sword is incredibly insightful. A sword is an implement of war. Isaiah said that one day God will bring absolute peace to this earth and men will beat *their swords*

57

into plowshares (Isaiah 2:4). The context of Isaiah 2:4 is about warfare and conflict. Therefore, we can see that the sword is a clear metaphor of warfare. We can see this principle fleshed out when Jesus was tempted in the wilderness by Satan. (Matthew 4:1-11). Each temptation or attempt to trip up Jesus was combated by a scripture that Jesus quoted back to the devil. The devil said, "Turn these stones into bread." Jesus replied, "It is written man does not live by bread alone but by every word that comes out of the mouth of God." (Matthew 4:4) Jesus is tempted by the devil three times in this passage in Matthew 4:1-11, but Jesus quotes the Bible in every response to the devil. Jesus' defense in warfare with the devil was connected to His intimate knowledge of the Hebrew scriptures. Jesus used the Bible to defeat His spiritual nemesis. Jesus was in warfare with the devil and He had a sword to defend Himself and obtain the victory over temptation and the deceit of the wicked one.

Do you remember the movie character Zoro? Zoro was a Spanish fictional character that was skilled at using his sword against many adversaries. He would whip out his sword and deftly make his signature "Z" on his opponent's chest. Believers in Jesus need to be like Zoro. We need to be able to skillfully deploy scripture against the attacks of the enemy of our souls. When we whip out God's word and flash it at the enemy, he is defeated and must flee from us (James 4:7-8).

GOLF CADDIES

When Paul says that the Bible is like the sword of the Spirit, he is reminding us that the Holy Spirit uses the Word of God in our defense when we are attacked. In other words, the Holy Spirit personally highlights and employs the scripture we need during times of crisis. I have already shared in this book how the Holy Spirit, at a certain dark time of my life, gave me a specific scripture to help me through a crisis. When Paul says that the Word of God is the sword of the Spirit, he is saying that the Spirit takes God's word that is hidden in our hearts, and brings it to our minds to protect us from spiritual attacks.

That spiritual attack may be a temptation, a time of depression, a time of discouragement, or the propensity to make poor decisions. In order to protect us from something destructive coming into our lives, the Spirit will bring to remembrance a scripture to aid us. That scripture may help keep us from sinning, sinking into despair, or from making a really bad decision. Jesus told His disciples that after He left, the Holy Spirit would bring back to their remembrance the things He had said to them (John 14:26).

The Holy Spirit is sort of like a golf caddy. If you are a professional golfer (which I am not) you have a caddy that walks beside you because he knows the course better than you do. When you reach certain places on the course, the caddy knows the surroundings, the impact of the wind, and how far you are from the pin on the green. He knows the right club you need to use in order to succeed. The Holy Spirit is our caddy in life. He places in our mind and heart the scripture that we need to succeed. In order to win in life, we need to fill our hearts and minds with God's word and allow the Holy Spirit to quicken and make alive the scriptures we need when we face different situations in life.

WHY PEOPLE DON'T READ THE BIBLE

As valuable as scriptures are, some people still don't have a daily habit of reading the scriptures. Some people don't read the Bible because they say that they hate to read. Now I understand this is a real problem for many people. I personally love to read. Now before you call me a nerd, let me tell you this about myself. I haven't always enjoyed reading. I hated to read in high school.

When I was in Bible College, I met a man named Carl Vincent who was full of wisdom. Karen and I used to enjoy going to his house and visiting with him and his wife, Phylis. During that important period in my life, he became my mentor and model of faith. I will always be grateful to Carl for his influence in my life.

Carl was always reading something. Whenever Karen and I would visit Carl and his wife, he would ask me, "What are you reading?" In those days all I was reading was the back of the cereal box in the morning when I was eating my breakfast, but Carl's lifestyle of reading inspired me. Carl was dedicated to reading and growing in knowledge. In fact, he and his wife didn't even have a TV; they would read at night instead of wasting their time watching sitcoms.

Carl was one of the wisest people I had ever met. One day it occurred to me that there must be a connection between Carl's great wisdom and his love of books. I started buying books and began to read like Carl; before long I was hooked on reading. Now I need to watch myself so I don't buy too many books. I am like that 16th Century scholar Desiderius Erasmus who once said, "When I get a little money I buy books; and if any is left I buy food and clothes." The point is that reading is an acquired taste.

I remember when I was young, I used to hate the taste of coffee. Then sometime during my college years, I began to drink a little coffee to stay awake to study for exams and slowly became addicted to it. Today I love coffee, but it was an acquired taste. Reading was the same for me; I gradually fell in love with it like I had with coffee.

Maybe I haven't convinced you that you could learn to love to read. Fair enough. If you can't imagine loving to read, you may be an audible learner. The great thing about our modern world is there are so many ways to listen to the Bible. For instance, the YouVersion of the Bible is an amazing tool. This app enables you to listen to the Bible anytime and in any version you choose. Sometimes I walk into the bathroom while my wife Karen is applying her make-up. While she goes about her morning routine, she has her iPad on the top of the vanity and listens to God's word. Karen is full of wisdom and has incredible peace regardless of what she goes through in life. I think her wisdom and her peace is directly connected to her listening to God's word every day. Regardless of your method of getting the word in you, fill yourself with God's word and you will be wise and full of peace.

I DON'T UNDERSTAND THE BIBLE

Some people say that they don't read the Bible because it makes no sense to them. One of the biggest objections of why people don't read the Bible is that they don't understand it. When I hear that, it makes me think of a quote by Mark Twain. Twain said, "It is not the parts of the Bible that I don't understand that trouble me it is the parts that I do understand!" I have often been told, "Pastor Danny, I don't read the Bible because I just don't understand it." Sometimes they will couch that statement in a compliment and add, "When you preach the Bible I understand it, but when I read it I don't understand it." I always feel good when people say they understand the Bible better when I preach it. However, I know that everyone needs to learn to read the Bible, as well as to listen to good teaching in their church.

The most important thing about understanding the Bible is understanding the context and the backstory of whatever book in the Bible you are reading. In other words, when reading through a book of the Bible, you need to know fundamentally what the book is about. If you don't know the big picture, the individual chapters of that book will make little sense to you.

THE BIBLE IS LIKE A PUZZLE

If you have ever bought a puzzle to put together for fun, you know the first thing you do is look at the picture on the box cover. You start with understanding the picture of what you are supposed to put together. It would be difficult to put a puzzle together if you had no idea what the puzzle was supposed to look like when it was completed. The individual pieces would make no sense because you wouldn't know what kind of picture you were creating. The books of the Bible are the same way. You need to know the big idea or picture of a book for the pieces to make sense. For instance, this week I read the book of Lamentations. I knew I was going to be lost if I didn't get some help understanding what the book was about. I listened to a short overview of Lamentations by the producers of the Bible Project on YouTube.

The Bible Project has produced multiple short videos overviewing many of the books of the Bible. You can go to https://bibleproject.com to access these videos, or you can just type in the name of the book you are reading on YouTube. Their videos and overviews of books of the Bible are amazing.

Another source that every Christ follower needs is a good Study Bible. Study Bibles come with an introduction to each book so you can see the overview of the book, and learn a bit about the author, the time, and the purpose of that book. In addition, each chapter of that book will have explanations in the footnotes regarding the most important verses in that chapter.

There are a variety of great Study Bibles. You can read reviews, or ask friends or your pastor to find the Study Bible that is right for you. As far as translations are concerned, many people read the English Standard Version or the New International Version. A good paraphrase version to read is the New Living Translation. I read the ESV, and supplement my study with the NIV and NLT.

Do Some Digging

When I was in Bible College, the man that taught me Greek and also taught many of the New Testament classes I took, was a man named Burl Bagwell. While studying one day, we came to this verse:

2 Timothy 2:15

"Study to shew thyself approved unto God, a workman that needeth not to be ashamed, rightly dividing the word of truth." KJV

I will never forget when Professor Bagwell told us that the word "study" means to "work hard." He told us that the word is *spoudazo* in the original Greek. Strongs Concordance says that *spoudazo* means: to make effort, be earnest or be diligent. Reading the Bible and growing in your faith involves discipline, effort, and commitment. After many decades of following Jesus, I can tell you that being committed to reading the Bible every day is worth the effort and commitment. I believe that your power, attitude, and the quality of life will radically improve as you put in the work to be a daily Bible reader.

Discussion Questions

1. How is the Bible like a GPS system? Why is the Bible particularly helpful during times of change?
2. How is Joshua and the Israelites following the ark of the covenant across the Jordan River a good illustration of keeping your eyes on God's word during times of change?
3. Why is the book of Proverbs particularly helpful with the practical issues of life?
4. If we hate to read, is there any hope for us that we could acquire an appetite for reading?
5. What's another way that we can take in God's word if reading is a problem for us?
6. If we don't understand the Bible, what are some of the resources that can use to assist us?

4

Hope: When Your Dreams are Delayed

"You are never too old to set another goal or to dream a new dream." – C.S. Lewis

Holding Patterns

I hate to wait. I once was flying back from a mission trip in Germany and had to change planes in London's Heathrow Airport. I was tired and ready to get back to the good ole USA to see my beautiful wife and family. As the plane approached London, the pilot came on the intercom and said there were some problems with the landing schedule for the runways at the airport, and we were going to have to stay in a holding pattern until we were cleared for landing. We were not the only plane in this predicament because when I looked out the window, I saw about a dozen planes surrounding us, all in holding patterns waiting to land. We waited for what seemed like an eternity and finally were given the go ahead to land. The delay made the connecting flight a challenge, but I eventually got home. Life is filled with holding patterns. I don't like them, you don't like them, but they are a part of everyone's life.

TRIVIAL THINGS WE HATE TO WAIT FOR

I hate to wait in grocery lines. I am one of those people that counts the items of the person in front of me in the express lane. The sign says *12 Items or Less* and I take that to be a literal number. Evidently, I am not the only person that wants that number enforced. However, the grocery store I frequent recently changed the sign to say, *"About 12 Items."* The word "about" is a pretty arbitrary word and makes it difficult to challenge the line hoarder in front of you.

I also hate waiting at traffic lights. Karen and I live near the beach in Delaware and the beach highway has tons of traffic lights. It seems that these traffic lights, when they turn green, are designed to let about a half car through before it turns red again! I cannot tell you how frustrated that makes me.

Doctor's offices are another place that can frustrate impatient people like me. My dermatologist is the worst. I can go into the waiting room for my appointment clean-shaven and have a Duck Dynasty beard when I leave! A study a few years ago concluded that the average person that goes to the emergency room must wait four hours and seven minutes. It seems we have forgotten the concept of "an emergency room."

I hate to wait at the baggage claim to get my luggage after a flight. When I get off the plane, I want my stuff so I can be on my way. My wife, Karen, is much better at waiting than I am; she is more patient. To be honest, she is more spiritually minded than I will ever be. She once stood in line at a store for two-and-a-half hours to buy her items. She loves to shop but this was even a stretch for her. However, she said she had some great deals and the wait was worth it. I would rather hurl myself into oncoming traffic than wait in line at a store that long. She had her sister with her during this shopping trip, so they chatted to make the time pass.

THINGS WE HATE TO WAIT FOR

There are other more important things in life that many of us don't enjoy waiting for. How about waiting for your body to recover from some sort of injury or medical procedure? I had knee surgery a few years back and couldn't play tennis or exercise for almost four months. I was required to do physical therapy, but as the weeks rolled by, it just seemed like my knee would never heal. Truth be told, it took about a year before my knee began to feel normal again.

Part of the reason for the delay in my healing was my age. When you get older it seems you heal slower. I don't like that reality, but it is a fact. When you are young, and in your twenties, you could cut your arm off and a new one would grow back by the morning! When you get a bit older, the healing process slows way down, and you need to wait for the muscles and the bones to mend.

Some people get weary in waiting for the right life partner to come along. They wait for Mr. Right or Miss Amazing to come along, but they see no real potential spouse on the horizon. Some people get impatient and lower their standards because they get tired of waiting for the right person. It's better to wait for the right person then to jump the gun and have the wrong person. I always say, "Be patient because it is better to want what you don't have than to have what you don't want!"

WAITING FOR PERSONAL CHANGE

If you are a serious follower of Jesus, maybe you are tired of waiting to be sanctified, to become more like Him. This is an area that I struggle with. I get so frustrated with myself when I slip into an old pattern that isn't Christ-like. I may be going along doing great and feel like my old, sinful struggles are gone forever, and then out of the blue, I find myself stumbling again.

I have a bit of a short fuse and have prayed about not being angry or edgy when things frustrate me. I have made a great deal of progress in this area but there are moments when my patience goes out the window and I fall into old, sinful patterns. Many serious Jesus followers have similar experiences. When this happens, I am always comforted by Philippians 1:6. This verse is my very favorite verse in the Bible. It says in part, "...he who began a good work in you will carry it on to completion until the day of Christ Jesus." Boy I love that verse. It both comforts and encourages me. God continues to change me, and He will finish the job. He will carry on His work in me until Jesus comes back to complete the job.

When Ruth Graham, wife of Evangelist Billy Graham, died a few years ago, she had this phrase put on her tomb stone: "Construction Complete; Thanks for your Patience." What a humorous epithet to put on one's tombstone. Her words are also very encouraging. Mrs. Graham was saying, "I am now with Jesus and I am totally sanctified." Her phrase "thanks for your patience", conveys she was surely not perfect in her life on earth, but now that she was with Jesus, she was perfect in every way.

One day you and I will be completely transformed and completely like Jesus. Jesus finished the job He began in Ruth Graham and He will finish the job He began in you as well. He will do that for all of us. Maybe you are tired of your bouts with your addiction and stumbling, but remember He is still working on you and He won't stop until He is done.

1 John 3:2

"Dear friends, now we are children of God, and what we will be has not yet been made known. But we know that when Christ appears, we shall be like him, for we shall see him as he is." NIV

You and I can be people of hope because the God who created the universe is incrementally changing us to make us more like His son. Be filled with hope because God will not quit; He will be persistent in changing you into a person of beautiful holiness.

NOAH A MAN THAT HAD TO WAIT

When I think of people that had to wait, I immediately think of Noah. He is infamous for building the giant ark that preserved his family and earth's animals from the great flood that God sent to judge mankind. We often miss the fact that Noah was in the ark for over a year. If you do the math, he was actually in the ark with his family for one year and ten days. That's a long, long time! We can calculate the length of time Noah was in the ark by paying attention to when he entered the ark and when he left the ark. Look at the details of these verses and calculate the time yourself:

Flood came **17th day of 2nd month** *of Noah's* **600 year**

Genesis 7:11

11 In the six hundredth year of Noah's life, on the seventeenth day of the second month—on that day all the springs of the great deep burst forth, and the floodgates of the heavens were opened. NIV

Noah left Ark **27th day of 2nd month** *of Noah's* **601 year**

Genesis 8:13-16

13 By the first day of the first month of Noah's six hundred and first year, the water had dried up from the earth. Noah then removed the covering from the ark and saw that the surface of the ground was dry. 14 By the twenty-seventh day of the second month the earth was completely dry.15 Then God said to Noah, 16 "Come out of the ark, you and your wife and your sons and their wives. NIV

Regardless of how you look at it, being in the ark for over a year is a very long time, especially to be confined in a limited space with one's family. We all love our families but too much togetherness can be challenging. Noah waited and waited and was certainly ready to get off the ark. In chapter eight we notice that Noah sent out birds to see if the land was dry enough for he and his family to leave the ark. This action of releasing the birds is repeated several times. This persistent bird-release-program reveals the great desire Noah had to get off the boat. Regardless of Noah's yearning to disembark, it should be noted that Noah did not get off the ark when the land was dry; he got off the ark when God told him to. Notice these important words:

Genesis 8:14-16

14 By the twenty-seventh day of the second month the earth was completely dry.15 Then God said to Noah, 16 "Come out of the ark, you and your wife and your sons and their wives. NIV

This is a powerful part of Noah's story. Noah was sensitive to the Holy Spirit. He doesn't do what his natural mind tells him to do — he patiently waits until the Lord gives him the nod to get off the ark. God ordained a specific day for he and his family to leave. There is a set, ordained day for that thing *you* are waiting for to come to pass as well. God has the appointed time for all your dreams to come to pass.

Our role is to wait on Him and trust in Him, and He will bring about that thing we are longing for at the right time. Naturally, we are to be diligent and proactive as well.

Noah was doing his part by sending the birds out to see if the land was dry. Noah did his research, but he waited until God gave him the green light to get off the ark. As you read the passage below you can almost feel the anticipation that Noah must have felt as he longed to get off the ark.

Gen 8: 6-12

6 "After forty days Noah opened a window he had made in the ark 7 and sent out a raven, and it kept flying back and forth until the water had dried up from the earth. 8 Then he sent out a dove to see if the water had receded from the surface of the ground. 9 But the dove could find nowhere to perch because there was water over all the surface of the earth; so it returned to Noah in the ark. He reached out his hand and took the dove and brought it back to himself in the ark. 10 He waited seven more days and again sent out the dove from the ark. 11 When the dove returned to him in the evening, there in its beak was a freshly plucked olive leaf! Then Noah knew that the water had receded from the earth. 12 He waited seven more days and sent the dove out again, but this time it did not return to him." NIV

Noah was in a holding pattern. He had to wait but it wasn't forever, and neither will it be for you. We can have hope because even though the thing we long for has yet to happen, God has a perfect timing to give us that which we greatly desire.

Isaac Waiting to Get Married

Another person that waited a long time like Noah was Isaac, the son of Abraham. Isaac was not waiting to get off a boat, but he was waiting to get married. His mother, Sarah, had recently died so Isaac was sad and lonely. One day he came out of his tent and looked up and saw a group of camels in the distance coming toward him. On one of those camels was Abraham's servant. This servant went east toward Persia (current Iraq) to find a bride for Isaac. As far as we know, Isaac was unaware of this. It is important to remember that God is at work on your behalf even when you are not aware of it. At times it may seem that God has forgotten us. However, it is important to remember that God is active even when we think He isn't.

As the camels came closer, Isaac could see a beautiful young lady with his father's servant. Her name was Rebekah. The Bible says that when she came toward Isaac, she got off her camel, and Isaac took her as his wife. Look at this beautiful passage:

Gen 24:62-67

62 Now Isaac had come from Beer Lahai Roi, for he was living in the Negev. 63 He went out to the field one evening to meditate, and as he looked up, he saw camels approaching. 64 Rebekah also looked up and saw Isaac. She got down from her camel 65 and asked the servant, "Who is that man in the field coming to meet us?"

"He is my master," the servant answered. So she took her veil and covered herself.

66 Then the servant told Isaac all he had done. 67 Isaac brought her into the tent of his mother Sarah, and he married Rebekah. So she became his wife, and he loved her; and Isaac was comforted after his mother's death. NIV

I once heard a minister speak on this passage as he sought to encourage the young singles in the crowd that were waiting for a spouse. The title of his message was, "The Camels are Coming!" Regardless of what you are waiting for, always remember the camels are coming. God will bring to you the desires He has put in your heart.

Isaac and Noah both were recipients of the thing that they both longed for. Noah longed to get off the boat onto dry land; Isaac desired a wife that he could love and spend time with. God had a specific timeframe for these things to happen for Noah and Isaac. Don't lose hope! When the desires of your heart are not being manifested, remember that you are not at the end of your story yet! In Noah's and Isaac's cases, their extended wait actually made the moment their dream was fulfilled even sweeter.

A BOAT WITHOUT A RUDDER

Let's return to Noah for a moment. Noah's long captivity in the ark was a time that he was completely powerless. I once studied the story about Noah and made an interesting discovery. There is a great deal of detail about how Noah was to build the ark. He was instructed how long, how wide, and how tall it was to be. He was even told what type of wood to use. God revealed that he should have an opening around the top of the ark, probably for ventilation. Here are some of the details of the construction of the ark:

Gen 6:14-17

14 So make yourself an ark of cypress wood; make rooms in it and coat it with pitch inside and out. 15 This is how you are to build it: The ark is to be three hundred cubits long, fifty cubits wide and thirty cubits high. 16 Make a roof for it, leaving below the roof an opening one cubit high all around. Put a door in the side of the ark and make lower, middle and upper decks. NIV

God is a detailed God and he gave Noah a very specific blueprint for the construction of the ark. The New Living Translation says that the ark was 450 feet long, 75 feet wide, 45 feet high, and it had 18 inches between the roof and the top wall of the ark. There is one thing that God did not tell Noah to build into the design of the ark. The missing element of the ark was a rudder; there was no way to guide or steer the ark. When we focus on the size of the ark, it's easy to miss the tiny detail that the ark was a rudderless vessel. The purpose of a rudder is to control and provide direction for a ship. The book of James says:

James 3:4

Or take ships as an example. Although they are so large and are driven by strong winds, they are steered by a very small rudder wherever the pilot wants to go. NIV

Noah was assumed to be the captain of the ark, but he had no way to steer this massive ship. The ark's design was solely for floating, not for guiding. In other words, God put Noah in a ship he could not control. God often puts us in situations that we cannot control. When we control our lives, we have no need to trust the Lord. When God allows us to be surrounded by circumstances that we cannot control, it forces us to surrender ourselves to Him. Peace comes not from being in control, but from knowing that God is in control. The longer I live, the more I realize that there are so many situations in life that I cannot control. God has put me in a boat without a rudder, countless times.

In Noah's case, he floated aimlessly around for months. After five months, the ark came to rest on Mount Ararat (Genesis 8:4). Noah didn't maneuver the boat toward Ararat; God sovereignly guided the ship to settle in that place.

Then Noah continued to wait. He and his family waited another seven months. While they waited, God began to cause the wind to blow in order to dry the land that had been covered by the water. The fact that the wind was acting like a gigantic blow dryer drying the land is insightful. I am not sure if Noah was aware that the wind was blowing, but it was blowing while he waited. The blowing of the wind was God drying the earth for Noah.

Genesis 8:1

But God remembered Noah and all the wild animals and the livestock that were with him in the ark, and he sent a wind over the earth, and the waters receded. NIV

Again, we need to remember that God is working on our behalf even if we are not aware of it. You may be sitting in a situation right now where you think you have no control.

We have all been there and will be there again in the future. If you listen closely, you will hear the wind blowing all around you. The sound of that wind means God is working on your behalf. He is working even if you are unaware of his providential activity on your behalf.

ZECHARIAH AND ELIZABETH

One of the greatest Biblical stories of waiting is the story of Zechariah and Elizabeth. You may recall hearing a message about them during the Christmas season. They were this older couple that were childless. Jewish culture believed that if a couple was childless, it must be symptomatic of an underlying issue in their lives. Barren women were thought to be cursed, as if there was a blemish or stain in their character, and the consequence was being unable to conceive. Naturally this was totally wrong, but it was what people in the ancient world believed. The writer of the gospel of Luke seeks to challenge this bogus view as he introduces the story to us:

Luke 1:5-7

5 In the time of Herod king of Judea there was a priest named Zechariah, who belonged to the priestly division of Abijah; his wife Elizabeth was also a descendant of Aaron. 6 Both of them were righteous in the sight of God, observing all the Lord's commands and decrees blamelessly. 7 But they were childless because Elizabeth was not able to conceive, and they were both very old.

Zechariah and Elizabeth were blameless. Now this doesn't mean they were perfect, but it does indicate that they were righteous people who walked morally and who were filled with integrity. Elizabeth and Zechariah were equally yoked and joined in Godliness and purity. It is important to remember that living for the Lord and walking in integrity doesn't mean that you will not suffer some deficits in your life. Zechariah and Elizabeth had so many positive things in their life. They had health even though they were advanced in years, they had a marriage filled with love, and they had the privilege of being from the priestly line of Israel to serve in the temple at Jerusalem. They had plenty of things that were good in their life, but there was one negative; Elizabeth was barren. It was this negative sign that brought Zechariah and Elizabeth so much pain.

When they were young, they dreamed of having children. Like most couples, being parents was high on their list of goals. Month after month, year after year, and decade after decade passed with almost no hope left. Zechariah and Elizabeth obviously prayed about this issue. We are not told how many times they prayed for a child, but at some point, they just gave up hope and quit praying. I have always wondered if their inspiration to pray for a child came from the book of Genesis. Here we have the story of Isaac and Rebekah. Rebekah was unable to conceive so the Bible says that Isaac prayed for Rebekah and she conceived:

Genesis 25:21

Isaac prayed to the Lord on behalf of his wife, because she was childless. The Lord answered his prayer, and his wife Rebekah became pregnant.

Perhaps Zechariah read that verse one day and shared it with Elizabeth. This story looked like the answer to their situation. It was so simple. Rebekah couldn't have a child, Isaac prayed, and Rebekah conceived. Have you ever gone to church and heard a sermon and the preacher made it sound so simple? A+B=C, right? Sometimes things in the Bible seem simple, but in real life they can be much more complicated. God had a purpose and plan for Isaac and Rebekah, but the plan and purpose God had for Zechariah and Elizabeth was different.

THE PURPOSE OF DELAYED PREGNANCIES IN SCRIPTURE

Often delayed pregnancies in the scriptures indicate that something significant was about to happen regarding God's plan of redemption for mankind. For instance, Abraham and Sarah waited and waited; Abraham was a hundred years old and Sarah was ninety-nine before they had the child God had promised them. What is significant about Abraham and Sarah is that they were the founders of what become the nation of Israel. It was through Israel that God would bring forth His Redeemer to purchase salvation for mankind. So, their delayed pregnancy had a redemptive connection and purpose. Revelation 12:1-5 describes a woman clothed with the sun and the moon. This imagery is borrowed directly from Genesis 37:9 and describes Israel as seen in a vision by Joseph. The author of Genesis describes Joseph's vision which points to the future nation of Israel:

Genesis 37:9

Then he had another dream, and he told it to his brothers. "Listen," he said, "I had another dream, and this time the sun and moon and eleven stars were bowing down to me." NIV

In this vision, the eleven stars represent Joseph's brothers, and they along with Joseph make up the twelve tribes of Israel.

Many years later, on the isle of Patmos, John receives the same vision of the woman clothed with the sun and moon and twelve stars. This is an obvious image of Israel. The astrologically-adorned woman gives birth to a son that will rule the nations. The son is a clear image of Jesus who was born an Israelite. When we condense the story, it goes like this: God founded Israel, and Israel brought Jesus into the world to redeem mankind. Revelation 12:1-5 says:

> *12 A great sign appeared in heaven: a woman clothed with the sun, with the moon under her feet and a crown of twelve stars on her head. 2 She was pregnant and cried out in pain as she was about to give birth. 3 Then another sign appeared in heaven: an enormous red dragon with seven heads and ten horns and seven crowns on its heads. 4 Its tail swept a third of the stars out of the sky and flung them to the earth. The dragon stood in front of the woman who was about to give birth, so that it might devour her child the moment he was born. 5 She gave birth to a son, a male child, who will "rule all the nations with an iron scepter." NIV*

Here is the point; the long wait that Abraham and Sarah endured to have Isaac was connected to a specific purpose and plan of God. That purpose was the constitution of Israel as a nation that led to Jesus coming to this planet to save us. The wait was ordained by God for His divine purpose. Likewise, when you are waiting for something that seems so far from happening, you may be a part of God's great story for your life, and even for His purpose and plan in divine history.

Sarah and Abraham's wait was providential because they were bringing forth a nation. Zechariah and Elizabeth's wait was part of God's purpose and plan because their child would baptize Jesus in the Jordan river. Their baby would be called John the Baptist, and he would become a significant actor in the story of redemption. Their wait had a divine purpose and plan and so does ours. So if you are waiting, don't give up hope because God is actively at work in your story.

Discussion Questions

1. Are you the kind of person that hates to wait for things? On a scale of 1 -10, how impatient are you in waiting for things that you want to happen but haven't happened yet?
2. When God told Noah to construct the ark, He gave him specific dimensions and details about how to build the ark. What is the one thing that God did not tell Noah to build into the ark?
3. How does this missing element illustrate that God sometimes places us in situations that we cannot control?
4. Noah was in the ark with his family for over a year. What was the final deciding factor that allowed him to leave the ark with his family?
5. When Noah was in the ark, the wind blew to recede the waters.
6. It is unclear if Noah was aware of this within the confines of the boat. Discuss the principle of how God is at work on our behalf even when we are

not aware of it. When God has us in a holding pattern while we wait, He always has a plan and purpose for the wait.

7. How does Abraham and Sarah waiting for a child confirm this principle?

5

BE A PERSON OF HOPE

"Human beings can live for forty days without food, four days without water, and four minutes without air. But we cannot live for four seconds without hope." Anonymous

Hope is Essential

Hope is not optional on this planet. Hope is essential. When you buy a new truck or car, some things are optional, and some things are essential. You can choose to have leather, heated seats, or you can opt for cloth seats to save money. (I highly recommend leather and heated seats). If you are buying a truck, you can select to have a running board to enhance the appearance of the truck, or you might bypass that option. However, the steering wheel is not optional for either a truck or car; it is essential.

Hope is like the steering wheel in life. We must have hope; it is not optional. If we lose our hope and become hostage to hopelessness, we are in serious trouble. Hope is the oxygen of life. We must breath in hope every day to survive the challenges of life that we are sure to encounter.

CIRCUMSTANCES CAN CRUSH OUR HOPE

It is easy to let the circumstances in life rob us of hope. If we lose hope, we must be careful that our hopelessness doesn't begin to spiral out of control and lead us into a dark, depressed place. Depression is the first cousin to hopelessness. I have felt hopeless at certain points in my life. When you are hopeless, you feel as if you are in a dark, black room with no windows, no doors, and no way to escape. However, according to God's word there is always a way of escape. (1 Corinthians 10:13). In this chapter we will discover how to overcome hopeless feelings, but first, we will learn a bit more about how hopelessness operates.

HOPELESSNESS IS CONTAGIOUS

I am writing this book during the COVID-19 pandemic. COVID-19 literally changed everyone's lives overnight. Each night we all gather around the TV to see how many infections were reported that day, and to see how many people filed for unemployment. I must confess that after a while I had to limit my news consumption. The avalanche of bad news was emotionally crippling for me. Unfortunately, the role of the nightly news in our culture is not merely to inform but to sensationalize the events of the day. Rarely is any good news cited, and many news people are prophets of gloom. The emphasis on this highly infectious virus reminded me that there is one thing that is more infectious than COVID-19—hopelessness. The most infectious thing in the world is not COVID-19, malaria, or chicken pox, it's hopelessness. If I am hopeless, I will be verbal about my hopelessness, and my words have the potential to affect others.

HOPELESSNESS CAN BECOME A PANDEMIC

Hopelessness is not just an individual thing; it can also be a collective experience. One hopeless person can infect people around them with their sense of despair and utter loss. When we allow hopelessness to debilitate us, we are in danger of letting it spread to our family, co-workers, and friends. Leaders must be especially careful to not let hopelessness cripple them and therefore spread to the teams they oversee. Leaders must also be diligent to not let hopelessness dominate their emotions publicly. It is important that we all spend time processing any feelings of despair with a pastor, close friend, spouse, or counselor. However, public venting is always problematic. Hopelessness is not a feeling we should share with the masses around us. During this pandemic, many are wearing masks and are practicing social distancing to protect others from the disease. The same care should be practiced with our emotions. I always cringe when people "tell all" on Facebook. Our emotional struggles are not for the general consumption, they are meant to shared only with a few, trusted, covenant friends.

KAREN'S SEASON OF DEPRESSION

Several years ago, my wife Karen went through a season of depression. This was extremely surprising because Karen had always been a very positive and upbeat person. In all the years that we had been married, I had never seen Karen depressed or filled with despair. Karen was the epitome of emotional steadiness.

During Karen's emotional crisis, a few, trusted, female friends came over weekly to talk, counsel, laugh, and pray with Karen. These four women loved Karen; they had been her friends for years. However, most of the people in our church and the general public were unaware that Karen was going through this tough time. I can still hear the sweet sounds of the prayers, laughter, and love of these dear friends coming from our den where they met to help support Karen. Karen was very blessed to have these precious ladies that loved her and supported her during her dark time. Karen processed her pain wisely with the right people. Hopelessness needs to be processed with the proper sources so we can receive the help we need while being careful not to infect those around us with our pain. The reasons for Karen's depression and hopelessness became clear after she sought counseling and met with her friends.

Karen was entering a new phase of life and her role as a hands-on mom was fading away as our sons got older. Karen had been an all-star mom whom our two sons leaned on and relied on during their first twelve to fourteen years of their lives. As they entered adolescence, their need for Karen shifted more to their friends and other authority figures. This transition affected Karen's emotions profoundly.

In addition to this life transition, we had walked through some difficult deaths at our church. Because of Karen's deep sense of compassion, she became overwhelmed. Coupled with her own internal pain, she also carried the grief of so many others; it was nearly more than her heart could bear. She pulled through that very difficult time with the help of few friends, prayer, and a good counselor. It's now been decades since Karen has experienced any depression. She processed with the right people and regained her emotional footing. Karen's struggle was private and handled with wisdom and care. Her season of darkness reminds me of the famous song by Twila Paris entitled the "Warrior is a Child"

Lately I've been winning
Battles left and right
But even winners can get
Wounded in the fight
People say that I'm amazing
Strong beyond my years
But they don't see inside of me
I'm hiding all the tears

They don't know that
I go running home when I fall down
They don't know Who picks me
Up when no one is around
I drop my sword and cry for just a while
'Cause deep inside this armor
The warrior is a child

Unafraid because His armor is the best
But even soldiers need a quiet place to rest
People say that I'm amazing
Never face retreat
But they don't see the enemies
That lay me at His feet

They don't know that I go
Running home when I fall down
They don't know Who picks me
Up when no one is around
I drop my sword and cry for...

As a mature and prudent person, Karen processed her struggles wisely. She is a leader in our church and with our children. Many look to her for support and strength.

All people of influence need to give themselves permission to struggle. They need to process those struggles with the right folks and accept the fact that they are human. One of the great downfalls of many leaders and people of influence is they forget that they are human.

REMEMBER THE POWER OF YOUR INFLUENCE

If a leader of a family, business, sports team, state, or country becomes publicly hopeless, the results can be devastating. When a leader falls apart, others may follow suit and things can get chaotic quickly. Single parents can feel overwhelmed, but they should be careful not to display their hopelessness in front of their children; this only creates further insecurity in their family. Like dominos falling in succession, if a leader becomes publicly hopeless, others will absolutely be affected. If a parent becomes hopeless, it can spread to their kids. If a coach becomes hopeless, it can be passed onto the team. If a CEO become hopeless, it can permeate an entire company. Political leaders can spread hopelessness to an entire county, state, or nation. Hopelessness must be addressed wisely lest our bleak emotional state impacts everyone around us.

EZEKIEL PRESENTS A PICTURE OF COLLECTIVE HOPELESSNESS

There is a poignant image in the Old Testament of collective hopelessness. In the book of Ezekiel, we see a picture of rampant despair. Ezekiel was a prophet to Israel during their time of captivity in Babylon (608-538 BC, Jeremiah 29:10). One day Ezekiel had a vision that captured the emotional state of the nation of Israel. Ezekiel saw a valley full of dry bones. God doesn't always explain the meaning of visions to prophets, but this time He gave the explicit meaning of the vision to Ezekiel. Notice what the vision means:

> *"Then he said to me: "Son of man, these bones are the people of Israel. They say, 'Our bones are dried up and our hope is gone; we are cut off.'"* Ezekiel 37:11

The bones represented the national attitude of Israel while they were in captivity in Babylon. Israel felt like there was no hope for the future. Their view was that they would never get out of Babylon. They would never return to their homeland; they were stuck with no way out.

What if this was good as it got?

There was a movie that came out in 1997 that starred Jack Nicholson. Nicholson played a neurotic, obsessive-compulsive author that was hostile to everyone around him, particularly to his homosexual neighbor in the apartment building where he lived. Nicholson's obsessive-compulsive demands were specifically annoying to a waitress (played by Helen Hunt) that waited on him each morning for breakfast at the local restaurant. The movie demonstrates how diverse people can learn to bond over their common struggles.

One day Nicholson is sitting in the waiting room of his psychiatrist and says to the others in the waiting room, "What if this is as good as it gets?" That isolated line becomes the title of the movie *As Good as it Gets!* Maybe you have wondered that yourself. What if my life today is as good as it will ever be? As we age, this becomes even more poignant as we reflect on our past while looking to an unknown future. This is Israel's state of mind in Ezekiel; what if living in Babylon is all there is? Is this as good as it gets?

HOPE IS NOT DENYING REALITY

God took Ezekiel and carried him among the bones in the valley. God wanted Ezekiel to assess the situation he and his nation were in. God carried Ezekiel back and forth through the whole valley so he could completely assess the situation. Ezekiel summarizes how God insisted that he see the real condition of the bones in the valley when he writes:

Ezekiel 37:1-2

1 The hand of the Lord was on me, and he brought me out by the Spirit of the Lord and set me in the middle of a valley; it was full of bones. 2 He led me back and forth among them, and I saw a great many bones on the floor of the valley, bones that were very dry. NIV

Recovering hope in your life is not a matter of denying reality. The first step in recovering your hope is to acknowledge the legitimate problems you are facing. Pretending they don't exist is denial.

Denial is a false reality that will eventually collapse on you. I love the story in the book of Genesis when Abraham and Sarah were childless. The Lord came to Abraham and said, "This time next year you and Sarah will have a child." Abraham doubted and even laughed at such a proposition, but it eventually came to pass. Sarah conceived and nine months later they had a baby boy named Isaac. Isaac's name actually means laughter, so God had the last laugh! The book of Romans gives a tiny commentary on this and says that Abraham was realistic about his and Sarah's physical condition:

Romans 4:18-22

18 Against all hope, Abraham in hope believed and so became the father of many nations, just as it had been said to him, "So shall your offspring be." 19 Without weakening in his faith, he faced the fact that his body was as good as dead—since he was about a hundred years old—and that Sarah's womb was also dead. 20 Yet he did not waver through unbelief regarding the promise of God, but was strengthened in his faith and gave glory to God, 21 being fully persuaded that God had power to do what he had promised. NIV

Romans says that Abraham faced the fact that both his and Sarah's bodies were as good as dead, yet he still believed his situation would change. Miracles happen when we acknowledge there is a real problem, and that we need God to help us. Miracles don't happen by denying reality, but by facing and turning our negative circumstances to the Lord.

APOLLO 13

When the Apollo 13 space craft was launched into space in April of 1970, it had a major malfunction with the oxygen tank. John (Jack) Swigert radioed back to the NASA Mission Control Center and said, "Houston we have a problem!" This is always our first step to overcome hopelessness. It is essential and imperative that we take a close look at reality and invite God into our disaster zone. Ezekiel stood in a valley of bones which was his disaster zone. We must recognize our disaster zone and call it what it is.

THE BASIS FOR ISRAEL'S HOPELESSNESS

Israel had real issues that laid the groundwork for her hopelessness. Here is what had happened to Israel: Israel's capital, Jerusalem, had been completely destroyed by the Babylonians (586-587 BC), her temple had been demolished, and the walls and gates of her capital city had been decimated. Nehemiah later described the situation in Jerusalem this way:

Nehemiah 1:3 and 2:17

3 They said to me, "Those who survived the exile and are back in the province are in great trouble and disgrace. The wall of Jerusalem is broken down, and its gates have been burned with fire." Nehemiah 1:3

17 Then I said to them, "You see the trouble we are in: Jerusalem lies in ruins, and its gates have been burned with fire. Come, let us rebuild the wall of Jerusalem, and we will no longer be in disgrace." Nehemiah 2:17

Jerusalem was the symbol of Israel's pride and joy but now it was nothing but a waste land. Her army was defeated so there was little prospect of Israel making a comeback and overthrowing the Babylonians. As Israel reflected on her situation, things looked very gloomy.

A DEVASTATING FIRE

I remember one day when Karen and I first began to pastor our church in Delaware, we got a call at the church office. A family in our church had experienced a horrible fire that destroyed their farmhouse. We jumped in our car and headed toward Selbyville, Delaware, where this family lived. Miles before we arrived, we could see the billows of black smoke ascending into the sky around their small farm. When we finally arrived, the house was surrounded by fire trucks with firemen frantically trying to douse the flames. Unfortunately, it was too late; the house was completely engulfed in flames. I will never forget seeing the wife collapse into her husband's arms with tears streaming down her face. She was so shocked by what was happening that her body was limp in her husband's arms. I can still remember that scene even though it happened over thirty-five years ago. Karen and I stood with this sad couple in a barn a distance from their burning house. They were devastated as they helplessly watched all their worldly possessions disappear into the flames.

The devastating feeling of this poor farm couple must have been similar to what Israel felt when she left Jerusalem to go into captivity. I can just imagine thousands of Israelites marching in formation toward Babylon. As they were carried into exile they saw the black smoke billowing up from the temple of their beloved Jerusalem. A later author in the Psalms would describe Israel's feelings in captivity:

Psalms 137:1-6

1 By the rivers of Babylon we sat and wept
when we remembered Zion.
2 There on the poplars
we hung our harps,
3 for there our captors asked us for songs,
our tormentors demanded songs of joy;
they said, "Sing us one of the songs of Zion!"
4 How can we sing the songs of the Lord
while in a foreign land?
5 If I forget you, Jerusalem,
may my right hand forget its skill.
6 May my tongue cling to the roof of my mouth
if I do not remember you,
if I do not consider Jerusalem
my highest joy. NIV

Israel in captivity had lost her hope. When the Babylonians mocked the Jews and said, "Sing one of the songs of your homeland," they refused. There was no song in her heart because Israel was without hope. Emily Dickinson expresses the emotional state of hopelessness in this short poem:

"Hope is the thing with feathers
That perches in the soul
And sings the tune without the words
And never stops at all."
    —Emily Dickinson
Hopelessness can rob us of the song in our heart

and take the twinkle out of our eye. The good news is that Israel's disaster zone did not last forever. God speaks to Ezekiel because things are about to change. Israel would not remain in her disaster zone forever, and neither will we live indefinitely in our personal valley full of dead men's bones.

WHEN THE WHITE HOUSE BURNED DOWN

During the War of 1812, the British invaded Washington, our beloved capital, and burned the White House down. President Madison and his wife, Dolly, were able to escape with their lives. However, the punitive action of the vindictive British torching the White House psychologically affected our young republic. Even in this tragic moment, there was flicker of hope for America's future. Before fleeing the White House, Dolly Madison, with the help of aids, unbolted a large canvas picture of George Washington from the wall of the White House. Saving the beloved picture of Washington was a small but powerful gesture to say this was not the end of the American story. Although James and Dolly Madison never lived in the White House again, it would eventually be rebuilt, and generations of executive leaders would live inside its hallowed walls.

Although Jerusalem and her temple had been destroyed, it would be rebuilt. Ezekiel's vision of the valley of dry bones symbolized the devastation of Jerusalem and her surroundings. However, the hopeless state of the valley of dry bones was about to change.

PROPHESY TO THE BONES

God told Ezekiel to do something that really seemed silly to him. If you follow the Lord long enough, He will tell you to do things that just don't make sense. He may tell you to tithe when finances are tight, to walk across a room and give an encouraging word to someone that you don't know very well, or He may tell you to enroll your child in a different school. There are all sorts of curve balls that the Lord throws us in our spiritual pilgrimage. God told Ezekiel to prophesy to the valley of dry bones. The book of Ezekiel records the event this way:

Ezekiel 37:4-8

4 Then he said to me, "Prophesy to these bones and say to them, 'Dry bones, hear the word of the Lord! 5 This is what the Sovereign Lord says to these bones: I will make breath enter you, and you will come to life. 6 I will attach tendons to you and make flesh come upon you and cover you with skin; I will put breath in you, and you will come to life. Then you will know that I am the Lord.'"

7 So I prophesied as I was commanded. And as I was prophesying, there was a noise, a rattling sound, and the bones came together, bone to bone. 8 I looked, and tendons and flesh appeared on them and skin covered them, but there was no breath in them. NIV

God had something for Ezekiel to do bring hope back into a hopeless situation. There is always something for us to do to revive our hope, even in seemingly hopeless situations. We should always partner with God in any endeavor that He wants to change. I once heard Oral Roberts say, "Without God, I cannot do it; without me, God will not do it." In the valley of dry bones things were about to change, but they would only begin to change when Ezekiel did his part. Ezekiel had to stand up and prophesy into a situation that looked far from promising. The book of Romans tells us that God can call things into being that did not exist. (Romans 4:17). It is the act of obedience to God that will ultimately change our circumstances. We shouldn't question what God is asking us to do; we should just do in faith what He tells us to do.

GO FISHING AGAIN

There is a great story in the book of Luke about Jesus asking Peter to do something that didn't make any sense to Peter. Remember, God will ask us at some point in our spiritual journey to do something that doesn't make any sense. Peter and his companions had been fishing all night and had caught nothing. Galilean fishermen usually did their fishing at night because their chances of success were greater at night. The text in Luke says that Peter and his fishing partners had fished all night long and had caught nothing. They were on the shore of the sea of Galilee washing their nets, and hoping to wrap up their activities so they could go home to get some sleep.

While they were cleaning their nets, Jesus borrowed one of their boats to teach the crowd. He then told Peter and his friends to get back in their boat and to cast their net into the sea. This made no sense for two reasons. First, they had just gotten off the lake with zero fishing success. Second, it made no sense as they had just finished cleaning their nets of seaweed and debris; the nets were clean and ready to be packed away. Here is how Luke records the story:

Luke 5:1-7

1 One day as Jesus was standing by the Lake of Gennesaret, the people were crowding around him and listening to the word of God. 2 He saw at the water's edge two boats, left there by the fishermen, who were washing their nets. 3 He got into one of the boats, the one belonging to Simon, and asked him to put out a little from shore. Then he sat down and taught the people from the boat.

4 When he had finished speaking, he said to Simon, "Put out into deep water, and let down the nets for a catch."

5 Simon answered, "Master, we've worked hard all night and haven't caught anything. But because you say so, I will let down the nets."

6 When they had done so, they caught such a large number of fish that their nets began to break. 7 So they signaled their partners in the other boat to come and help them, and they came and filled both boats so full that they began to sink. NIV

The turning point in the story is when Peter says to Jesus, "Master, we've worked hard all night and haven't caught anything. But because you say so, I will let down the nets." I love Peter's attitude here. Sometimes we beat up on Peter for all his mistakes, but this is a moment when he was at his best. Peter loaded his clean nets and dragged his weary body into the boat to go fishing with Jesus.

On the very first cast of the net, and right where Jesus told him to throw it, Peter landed a huge catch of fish. At that moment Peter knew he was seeing a bonafide miracle right in front of his eyes. It was because of Peter's simple obedience to do his part that this amazing intervention of the Lord occurred. For Peter, it was putting the clean nets in the boat and pulling his weary legs over the side of the boat, that make this amazing thing happen. For Ezekiel, it was his obedience to speak to the valley of bones in faith. In each case a miracle occurred. Miracles always flow out of some form of obedience. When we do our part, God pours out His miraculous power to create hope in a world of hopelessness.

PASSIONATE ACTION

When I think of this scene and Ezekiel prophesying to skeletons on a valley floor, I wonder how passionate he was about speaking to scattered bones in the dirt? Was he ho-hum? Was he passionate with his words? We don't get any sense of this in the text. I think we sometimes start out in obedience, with little feeling or passion, but the longer we move in that obedience, the more excited we become in the process of doing our part in bringing a miracle into fruition.

I once had a wonderful guy on my staff named Andy. He was over our media department and was extremely talented. He was in his mid-twenties. He had finished his education, was working full time for our church, and was looking for a wife. Andy was a great guy, but he just couldn't find the right girl to settle down with. Then one year I scheduled a New Year's Eve party for the church. For some reason the younger members of our staff were not too excited about being a part of this event. Andy, who normally had a great attitude, was ill disposed toward this event. He shared with another staff member named David that he didn't want to go to this New Year's Eve event, and that he was really struggling with his attitude about having to go as a staff member to interact with the congregation at this party. David told Andy, "I know you don't want to do this, but Pastor Danny wants us to do this. So, let's do it and have a good attitude. Even if you don't want to go to the party, try to have a good attitude." Then he added, "Andy, be the party!"

At the event, Andy was sitting at the table with all the other young staff members that didn't want to be there. He got up to get some punch and walked by David's table. David said to him again, "Andy be the party!" Andy got out on the dance floor, danced a bit, and started to have a good time. He noticed a beautiful girl with brunette hair dancing on the other side of the dance floor; he'd never seen this young woman before. Later that night when the disc jockey played the chicken song, Andy was able to interact with this girl. It turned out that she didn't come to our church but had been invited to the party by someone from our church. After the night was over, Andy got the young lady's number from someone who knew her.

The following week he called her and asked her out for a date. The girl's name was Logan. One date turned into two, and two into three, and a few months later, Andy and Logan were married. Ironically, we have never had another New Year's

Eve party since that night when Andy met Logan.

Sometimes we have to get a good attitude even if we don't feel like it. Being obedient in something that we don't like doing can often bring a miracle. It may be throwing a net out of boat, yelling at dead bones, or going to a New Year's Eve Party. Either way, little steps of obedience can bring about miraculous results.

Discussion Questions

1. Why do you believe hope to be essential for life?
2. Why is it essential that we accept the fact that we *do* have problems and that we need God to help us? How did Abraham illustrate this as he considered the real condition of his and Sarah's bodies as they longed to have a child?
3. Why did the Lord have Ezekiel go up and down the entire valley inspecting the bones that were dry and lifeless? What was God wanting Ezekiel to realize?
4. Ezekiel's prophesying to the bones represent his part in the miracle that was about to take place. Discuss the principle: "We always have a part to play in every miracle God performs."
5. Sometimes God asks us to do things that do not make sense at the time. How does Peter's casting his clean nets back into the sea at Jesus' command illustrate this? Discuss the principle that obedience sometimes must be done by faith before we are excited about it.

6
Hope: Positive Environments

*"Keep your face to the sunshine
and you cannot see a shadow." Helen Keller*

Everyone who wants to be a person of hope must have a positive environment as a resource to fuel their hope. In other words, we draw our hope from being planted in the right environment. There is an incredible Psalm that gives us some guidance and insight on this idea. Here is how this Psalm reads:

Psalms 92:12-15

12 The righteous will flourish like a palm tree, they will grow like a cedar of Lebanon; 13 planted in the house of the Lord, they will flourish in the courts of our God. 14 They will still bear fruit in old age, they will stay fresh and green, 15 proclaiming, "The Lord is upright; he is my Rock, and there is no wickedness in him." NIV

You have got to love this Psalm. It talks about flourishing. Now I don't use the word flourishing very often— honestly, I never use it—but it is a great word. It means "to break forth with life." I want my life to break forth with abundance, and I know you do as well. Jesus alludes to the fact that we are to overflow with His abundant life while we are on the earth when He said:

John 10:10

10 The thief comes only to steal and kill and destroy; I have come that they may have life, and have it to the full. NIV

Why Are We Here?

Psalms 92 really captures why we are on this earth. Have you ever asked yourself why you are here on this place called earth? I remember sitting in a small pentagon shaped building in Bible College, waiting for a wedding to start. The little chapel where we were seated had a padded bench that went completely around the perimeter of the room. There were about twenty-five or thirty people sitting in the chapel, facing each other in awkward silence. The tiny wedding party, along with the staff minister that was performing the ceremony, had not arrived yet. The senior pastor of the church, Ken Sumrall, was also sitting in the small group waiting for the ceremony to begin. As we all sat there together, Pastor Ken felt the awkwardness that we all were experiencing. Pastor Ken broke the silence and said, "Does anyone know why we are here?" His humorous remark made everyone laugh and the awkwardness dissipated. His humorous question is the real question all of us should ask about life. "Why are we here?"

THE INSIGHT OF PSALMS 92

According to Psalms 92 we are on this earth to flourish. The psalmist says that the righteous will be like palm trees and cedar trees (Psalms 92:12). Each of these trees are known for their strength and beauty. The palm tree is known for bearing fruit. There are about 2500 different kinds of palm trees and they all bear some sort of fruit. Some palm trees produce dates, others produce betel nuts, and some produce special oils that have many beneficial uses. When the psalmist uses the palm tree as a metaphor for an abundant life, he is conveying that it is God's will that we become fruitful and productive in life. I believe God wants us to fruitful, strong, beautiful, and productive for our entire lives. Jesus said to his disciples, "It is my will that you go and bear much fruit." (John 15:8) How are we supposed to flourish in our lives? The Psalm gives some specific guidance on this important question.

BE RIGHTEOUS

First, we must be righteous. Maybe you think you could never flourish because you are so unrighteous. If you just knew the real me, you would know I am far from being righteous! I make mistakes and sin every single day. You may feel like your life is defined by inconsistency. James 3:2 begins with, "We all stumble in many ways."

There are really two types of righteousness: imputed righteousness and practical righteousness. The first kind, "imputed righteousness," is the righteousness that is given to us instantly when we put our faith in Jesus. This type of righteousness is a gift from God. It allows all who believe on Jesus the right relationship with God and eventually, the right to go to heaven to experience eternal life. Here is the amazing, crazy, and unbelievable thing about imputed righteousness. When we receive this gift of imputed righteousness, we are just as righteous as God himself! That sounds almost like heresy, but it is true. You and I, who are believers in Jesus, have the same level of righteousness that God has. Here are some scriptures to substantiate this claim:

2 Corinthians 5:21

God made him who had no sin to be sin for us, so that in him we might become the righteousness of God. NIV

What is amazing about this verse is that it says that because Jesus became sin for us, we then became "the righteousness of God." I have read this verse for years and years and have failed to really notice that phrase. Sometimes we can be so fixated on finishing a chapter in the Bible in our devotions, that we fail to slow down and see the words that are so important. That phrase, "become the righteousness of God," means that we have the same kind of righteousness that God has. In other words, when we receive Jesus, we are as righteous as God is. Bottom line, you and God have the same status of righteousness. The truth is, God doesn't have a superior righteousness than His believers;

106

we are all just as righteous as God. This concept of being just as righteous as God is also underscored in the book of Romans:

Romans 1:17

For in the gospel the righteousness of God is revealed—a righteousness that is by faith from first to last, just as it is written: "The righteous will live by faith." NIV

Paul says in this passage that in the gospel, the righteousness of God is revealed. Here is that phrase again: "the righteousness of God." This describes the type of righteousness that we receive when we accept the gospel (the good news of Jesus sacrificial death for us). We can flourish when we recognize that we are totally righteous in God's eyes. Paul often addressed the saints of the churches he had established. He wasn't inferring that they would be saints in the future; they were already saints. Did you know that you are a saint right now? Yes you! You are a saint. Notice what Paul said to the churches of Ephesus and Philippi:

Ephesians 1:1

Paul, an apostle of Christ Jesus by the will of God,

To the saints who are in Ephesus, and are faithful in Christ Jesus: ESV

Philippians 1:1

Paul and Timothy, servants of Christ Jesus, To all the saints in Christ Jesus who are at Philippi, with the overseers and deacons: ESV

Pastor Jack Hayford was once speaking on the theme that we are saints right now. He had everyone in his congregation turn to the person next to them and say, "Hi! I am Saint so and so (they inserted their name)." Scores of people turned and said, "Hi! I am Saint Fred" or, "Hi! I am Saint Barbara." One guy refused to do it. When the person next to him asked why, he said, "My name is Bernard." The poor guy just couldn't bring himself to say, "I am Saint Bernard." We can be people of hope because we have been made just as righteous as God.

PROGRESSIVE RIGHTEOUSNESS

The second type of righteousness is progressive righteousness. This is a type of righteousness that is gradually worked out in our life. We become more and more like Jesus the longer we live. As we apply ourselves to God's word and Christian fellowship, we are progressively changed. Imputed righteousness happens instantaneously while progressive righteousness (also called sanctification) happens over a lifetime, only to be completed at our death or the second coming of Jesus. (1 John 3:2) Paul said to the Philippian believers that they were to work out their salvation with fear and trembling. Paul doesn't mean that we need to work in order to receive salvation, he is merely saying that the gift of God's righteousness is to be "worked out" in our practical life. Look at Philippians:

Philippians 2:12-13

12 Therefore, my dear friends, as you have always obeyed—not only in my presence, but now much more in my absence—continue to work out your salvation with fear and trembling, 13 for it is God who works in you to will and to act in order to fulfill his good purpose. NIV

This verse implies something powerful. It underscores the fact that God, and we, are partners in the production of righteous living in our lives. We are told to "work out our salvation," but the verse also says that God "works in us." We can have hope because as we incorporate God's word into our daily life, God helps us to become more and more practically righteous. Greg Laurie of Harvest Church in San Diego, California says of this verse, "God wants us to work out what he has worked in." Laurie compares "working out our salvation" to the gold rush in California in the early 1800s. He said, "Just as the miners worked or mined for gold out of the earth of California during the gold rush we need to work out the spiritual gold that God has planted in us through the gift of our salvation."

Planted in the House of the Lord

Psalms 92 says that the righteous will flourish because they are planted in the house of the Lord and the courts of our God:

Psalms 92:13

planted in the house of the Lord, they will flourish in the courts of our God.

For us to flourish and thrive, we need to be planted in the house of God. So many people today are not planted in a good church. They are inconsistent; they hop around and never settle in a good Bible-believing and Jesus-loving church. This is not the way to flourish spiritually. The best way to flourish spiritually is to put your roots down in a good Bible-believing church.

In my backyard I have two gorgeous golden oak trees. These trees are huge. When Karen and I built this house about eighteen years ago, a kind lady in our church gave us $1000 at a local nursery for landscaping. Wow! I could do some serious landscaping with $1000. Turns out landscaping is expensive, and I could afford only two trees for my backyard. When the landscaping company delivered these trees, they were about seven feet tall — just a bit over my head.

Now, after eighteen years, these trees are huge. These magnificent trees ascend forty to fifty feet in the air. Both trees produce a large section of shade in my backyard during certain times of the day. The growth of these trees is directly related to the fact that they have been in one place, planted in my backyard, for eighteen years. Healthy believers are like big healthy oak trees. When we put our roots deep, and are "planted in the house of the Lord", we will flourish and grow. There is no spiritual growth without being planted in a spiritual community.

DO I HAVE TO GO TO CHURCH TO BE A CHRISTIAN?

I once had a man visit my church who indicated I said something in my sermon he didn't like. Good preaching sometimes needs to challenge people. One pastor said, "My job is to comfort the afflicted and afflict the comfortable." Evidently this particularl

Sunday I had done my job. I was preaching on Acts 16 and the conversion of Lydia. In the text it says:
Acts 16:13-15

13 On the Sabbath we went outside the city gate to the river, where we expected to find a place of prayer. We sat down and began to speak to the women who had gathered there. 14 One of those listening was a woman from the city of Thyatira named Lydia, a dealer in purple cloth. She was a worshiper of God. The Lord opened her heart to respond to Paul's message. 15 When she and the members of her household were baptized, she invited us to her home. "If you consider me a believer in the Lord," she said, "come and stay at my house." And she persuaded us. NIV

What I found intriguing about this passage is Lydia's insistence that Paul and his companions come to stay at her house after she was converted and baptized. Why was she so insistent that Paul and his friends come and stay with her? She was emphatic, "Come and stay .... and she persuaded us." I said in the sermon that she was insistent because as a new believer, she was hungry to grow in her faith and had a thousand questions for Paul and his team. The first evidence of her conversion was that she was hungry for spiritual things, and she wanted to be taught and have fellowship with other believers.

Then I said something controversial. A good sermon has at least one controversial statement which makes people say, "No way!" I proceeded and said, "You don't have to go to church to be a Christian, but if you are a Christian you will want to go to church." Truly regenerated (saved and born again) people have a spiritual passion to have fellowship with other believers, and a desire to grow in their faith. Jesus said, "Blessed are those that hunger and thirst for righteousness for they will be filled." (Matthew 5:6)

My controversial statement upset the man who was visiting our church. He was there because we had an infant dedication that Sunday and he was related to the family of the child. The gentleman was offended because he was a church hopper. He would attend different churches indiscriminately about every three months. He wouldn't go to church for weeks at a time but would then get a hankering to hear a certain preacher and would drive to that church in hopes of hearing an interesting sermon. Then he may not go to church for another couple of months but then spontaneously decide to visit another church. He was not unlike someone who would get an urge for Mexican food, Italian food, or sushi, and then randomly go to the restaurant that met their current appetite.

He made an appointment with me and told me about his pattern of church attendance. I was pastoral and kind to this spiritual nomad, but knew he needed to be challenged. I told him, "The kind of spiritual roaming around you are describing is foreign to the New Testament." I paused and continued, "There is nothing even remotely close to your church-attending patterns found in the Bible."

Paul wrote to the churches at Ephesus, Colossae, and Philippi. He wrote to groups of people that had found Jesus and regularly met together for teaching and fellowship. In Hebrews it warns against becoming undisciplined and for ceasing to attend church. This is probably one of the most well-known verses on church attendance. We should not let its familiarity rob us of the powerful challenge it presents. The writer to the Hebrews says:

Heb 10:24-25

24 And let us consider how we may spur one another on toward love and good deeds, 25 not giving up meeting together, as some are in the habit of doing, but encouraging one another—and all the more as you see the Day approaching. NIV

I finally said to the man, "If you go to heaven it will be so strange and weird to you." He asked what that meant, and I asserted, "Heaven is a place of corporate worship. It's groups of people serving and loving Jesus together. Heaven is not about one person wandering off by themselves to worship in isolation; heaven is about spiritual community." What I was trying to convey to this man was that when we have fellowship on earth with other believers, we are really practicing for eternity because eternity will be a forever spiritual-community with other believers. I finally prayed with the man, but he left still struggling with the idea that we are supposed to be "planted in the house of the Lord." Psalms 92 expresses the idea that in order to be fruitful, in order to flourish in life, one must be planted in the house of the Lord. I have been a pastor for almost forty years and have never seen a truly fruitful and vibrant Christian who was not planted in a spiritual community. We cannot grow in isolation, but when we are planted in the house of the Lord we will flourish.

GEORGE FRIEDEL

I was in a restaurant the other day with my dad when a very old man walked by. He looked familiar and I asked my dad if it was George Friedel. My dad answered and confirmed it was. George Friedel had been a part of my dad's church for decades. George was ninety-five years old at the time of this writing. George's table at the restaurant was only a few feet from our table so my dad and he began to talk and joke with each other. Dad has been George's pastor for over forty years. They are deep brothers and friends in Christ. I watched George smile and laugh as he and my dad enjoyed each other's company. George is one of the strongest and steadiest people of faith I know. I have known him since I was a young boy and he has always sported a smile and generous laugh.

His life hasn't been easy. His wife, Ida Mae, died of Alzheimer's disease a few years back, and his beloved son, a very influential minister, died unexpectedly several years ago. I have watched George weather storms, but he is like a cedar tree, standing tall and straight regardless of what he had gone through. What is George's secret? I think it has to do with his love for the church and his love for God's word.

I preach at my dad's church three or four times every year. I have done this for many years. I have never preached at my dad's church where George was not sitting in the third row to my left from the podium. He always comes into church carrying his well-worn Bible. I believe there is a direct correlation between George's joy, his smile, and his church attendance — even in adversity. Because George is planted in the house of the Lord, he flourishes regardless of what he is going through. No doubt George has grieved and been saddened by great losses in his life, but his spiritual roots, being deep in the courts of the Lord, have sustained him and made him full of life despite his circumstances.

FULL OF SAP AND FLEXIBLE

Psalms 92:14 says that the righteous will be like trees that are green and full of sap: They will still bear fruit in old age, they will stay fresh and green, NIV

One of my favorite translations of the Bible is the English Standard Version. It translates this verse this way:

They still bear fruit in old age; they are ever full of sap and green, ESV

Those that are planted in the house of the Lord will be "full of sap." Trees that have an abundance of sap in them can be extremely flexible. Trees that are not full of sap are brittle, rigid, and prone to snapping in two. When a tree has plenty of sap it can bend with the winds that come its way.

I once was invited to speak at a Youth with a Mission (YWAM) school in Jamaica. The speaking engagement was in February, and the thought of leaving frigid Delaware to be in Jamaica for a week during the dead of winter made the decision easy. I prayed about this invitation for about a millisecond and then agreed to go. The camp was filled with beautiful palm trees which were very tall. The administrator of the camp told me that during the fierce tropical storms that occasionally hit Jamaica during hurricane season, these palm trees are so flexible that as they are engulfed in the fierce winds, they can completely bend so that the top of the tree touches the ground. Now that is flexibility! The abundance of the sap in these palm trees gives them the capacity to adapt to the storm, and bend so that they don't break in two. The righteous, according to Psalms 92;14, have that same capacity.

OLD AND CRANKY

It seems to me that when we get older, we become more irritable and frustrated with the hassles of life. In HOA meetings, seniors are sometimes the most disagreeable people in the group. Even trivial things seem to annoy and bother them. Perhaps it is the wear and tear of the years that make many seniors become irritable and rigid; perhaps it is the boredom of retirement. Whatever the reason, longevity in life seems to make some people difficult to deal with.

I was standing in line the other day at BJ's Department store. The line was enormously long. There were about thirty to thirty-five people in front of me so I was going to be waiting for a while. An older gentleman came toward me at the end of the line. He was pushing a flatbed cart that was covered with merchandise. He said, "I can't believe how long this line is! This is the second time today I have had to wait in line here." My first thought was, "Why in the world would you come back a second time to wait in line?" For whatever reason he wanted me to know how frustrated he was. I didn't say anything. It occurred to me as he was unloading his frustration, that we are so blessed to have stores filled with merchandise of every kind in this country. If you have traveled abroad, you know that there are many third world countries whose shelves are virtually empty. Their problem is not waiting in line — it is scarcity. If I had to choose between one or the other, I would choose waiting any day. Unfortunately, the man venting on me was frustrated and inflexible regarding his situation.

Psychologist Henry Cloud once said, "Immature people insist that life meet their demands. Mature people meet the demands of life." It is important that we make the adjustments in our attitude in life rather than living with some illusion that our griping and complaining will change anything. I have decided that as I age; I want to have more grace and more patience rather than less. Again, I see grace and patience in my dad.

The other night we were at his favorite restaurant again and I noticed how flexible and undemanding he was. He was content with the booth, the quality of the food, and the service. He smiled and joked during the whole meal. As I looked around the restaurant, I saw many people in my dad's age group who had sour and grim expressions on their faces. Their faces seemed to signal their anger and frustration with life. I turned back to my dad and looked at a face, serene and happy. My dad has peace and joy. His life is not perfect, but he chooses to trust God and be flexible when life is demanding. Seeing his face gives me hope for my future.

Discussion Questions

1. What does it mean, according to Psalms 92, to flourish? What are the things necessary to incorporate into one's life in order to flourish?
2. What does it mean to be righteous? What are the two types of righteousness?
3. What does the phrase "the righteousness of God" mean and what are the implications of that phrase?
4. Why are authentic believers naturally drawn to Christian community and fellowship? How does Lydia in Acts 16 illustrate this?
5. When Psalms 92 speaks about the palm trees being full of sap, what is the implication of that phrase? Why are we more rigid as we get older?

7

HOPE IS POSSIBLE: WHERE HISTORY IS HEADED

"I'll go anywhere as long as it is forward."
David Livingston

Reincarnation and Stair Machines

Some religions are cyclical in nature. Life, according to some ancient faiths, is filled with reincarnations and rebirths. I don't mean to be critical of the fine people involved in these belief systems, but the idea of perpetually going in a circle makes me dizzy as well as hopeless. According to these eastern religious systems, life is a big repeating cycle that goes around and around.

I remember when I was in elementary school that my favorite item on the playground was the merry-go-ground. As soon as recess began, my friends and I would make a beeline right to the merry-go-round. We would latch onto it and get it moving rapidly in its circular orbit. After achieving maximum momentum, we would hang on, spinning, until we were lightheaded and dizzy.

Many current world views, many rooted in the East, have a merry-go-round view of history. According to these folks, we really aren't going anywhere; we are just staying in the same place and moving circularly through history as time passes. The groups that subscribe to reincarnation and a cyclical view of history are stuck in repeating life cycles that leave them stranded in time. According to these religious systems, only a few extremely elite people ever break free from the repetitive cycle of a dismal existence. The human heart and mind are designed to make progress.

The gym that my wife Karen goes to has a stair-climbing machine. This piece of equipment is torturous and brutal. I have gone to the gym with Karen but can only last about ten minutes on this beast before I have to jump off. Whoever invented this is certainly in an elite group of cruel and sadistic people. The most frustrating thing about the stair climber is that you must exert great effort to go absolutely nowhere. Metaphorically from a Biblical view, history is NOT a stair climber that will leave the human race exhausted and stuck in one spot. History is headed toward something incredible.

PROCESSIONARY CATERPILLARS

This cyclical philosophy in life reminds me of the processionary caterpillars researched by the scientist, Jean Henri Fabre. Fabre took a significant group of processionary caterpillars and put them on the ledge of a flowerpot. He placed all the favorite foods of these hairy little insects in the pot. However, the processionary caterpillars continued to go in a circle, faithfully following their caterpillar buddy in front of them. According to Fabre, they did this for over a week until one by one they began to die. Ironically, all their favorite foods were easily within reach within the flowerpot, but they continued their faithful suicide march around the ledge of the pot. In life, it is difficult to have hope if you do not believe that history is heading somewhere.

DREAMS AND GOALS AS WE MOVE IN A POSITIVE DIRECTION

Individuals that struggle with addictions and alcoholism often lack a goal or dream to keep them away from their bad habit. There may be other factors, but a large component of the problem has to do with a lack of vision for the future. If you are reaching for something good, it will keep you from reaching for something bad. It is amazing what a goal will do for a person. When you have something to reach for, you have hope. When you have hope, you are less likely to be depressed, and you are less prone to use drugs or your stimulation of choice. When we step back and realize that God has a purpose and plan for history, and we are not just poor, senseless souls going in a circle, we can be filled with hope; we are actually headed somewhere!

This view of history is called the linear view. A linear view of history can be illustrated by an ascending straight line that is constantly moving forward. In Proverbs it says, "The path of the righteous is like the light of dawn shinning brighter and brighter until the full day." (Proverbs 4:18) The writer of Proverbs says that a righteous person is like a beautiful day that begins with a sunrise and gets brighter and brighter like a sun rising in the sky toward high noon. This view of history is the basis of our hope for tomorrow.

THE SECOND COMING OF JESUS

The grand climax of history according to the New Testament, is the second coming of Jesus. There is a huge gap between where the Bible says history is ultimately heading and where the secular world says we are going. According to many scientists, the sun will one day die. As it explodes, becomes a red giant, it will vaporize everyone and everything on the earth. The only good news, from a scientific perspective, is this will not likely happen in our lifetime. Scientists estimate this will not happen for seven or eight billion years. However, this looming reality hangs over humanity like a bad headache.

The Bible, on the other hand, has a different view of where history is going. According to the Bible, Jesus is coming to set up His perpetual reign here on the earth. What will the conditions be like on the earth after Jesus takes total control? Here are just a few examples. Every war will be suspended and there will never be another. Every disease will disappear, putting hospitals and funeral homes out of business. Financially, everyone will prosper. In the end, according to scripture, the Lord will put to right everything which is not right. This view of history is so encouraging to me. It is hard to be a fatalist when you see God's ultimate plan for history and mankind. The Bible is the most optimistic book every written because it ends with all tears and pain eradicated from our planet (Revelation 21:4). How's that for hope?

One of the saddest things I have had to do as a pastor is to conduct funerals for young people who overdosed. I was called out one evening to a home to help a family that had found their son deceased because of a drug overdose. I comforted them as best I could. I let them know that they were loved and that their spiritual community would gather around them to support them. Unfortunately, this was not the only time I had to do this. Drugs will always be a problem in a world that believes that there is no purpose or plan for the future. Humans are purpose-based creatures that must believe that they are part of the great story God is writing.

THREE FEATURES OF HISTORY UNDER GOD'S RULE

There are three features of the ultimate future we are moving toward:

1. Peace and order
2. Righteousness over evil
3. Massive productivity and prosperity

Several scriptures support these aspects of our collective future.:

Isaiah 2:3-4

3 Many peoples will come and say, "Come, let us go up to the mountain of the Lord, to the temple of the God of Jacob. He will teach us his ways, so that we may walk in his paths."

The law will go out from Zion, the word of the Lord from Jerusalem. 4 He will judge between the nations and will settle disputes for many peoples. They will beat their swords into plowshares and their spears into pruning hooks. Nation will not take up sword against nation, nor will they train for war anymore. NIV

When you read these verses, you cannot help but be encouraged. In a world of political corruption and disarray, Isaiah says that one day the Lord will rule from His holy mountain. People from all over the globe will submit to His rule. His rule will result in the total elimination of war and conflict. Isaiah says, "They will beat their swords into plowshares." In a practical sense these words mean that war will be non-existent. Rioting and racial conflict will be a thing of the past. Jesus will make this crooked world straight again. We should be the proponents of justice in our time, but the reality is we will always fall somewhat short of achieving complete justice. We can start the process, even continue the process, but only Jesus will finish the process. Jesus' rule is inevitable and will make this planet like the garden of Eden again. History will not end with an exploding and dying sun, but with the reign of the Son.

CONFLICT OVER THE DETAILS

The New Testament is filled with references to the second coming of Jesus. This future event should fill our present time with hope. Christians often argue and debate about how and when the second coming of Christ will occur. This, however, is not the tone of the New Testament. The emphasis of the New Testament is that history is moving toward a grand conclusion. There are huge debates about if Jesus is coming before a tribulation period of seven years (Pre-Tribulation). Some believe He is coming after the first three-and-a-half years of the seven-year tribulations (Mid-Tribulation). Others believe it will be at the end of the seven-year tribulation period (Post-Tribulation). Another group believes there will be a one-thousand-year millennium of peace after the tribulation period, while others believe that the concept is just metaphorical, and we are living in the millennium now. Honestly, I love studying these various views. I find the subject fascinating.

I have also discovered that there are equally brilliant and sincere people who adopt to each of these seemingly conflicting views. One gentleman when asked about his eschatological position said, "I am a pan-millennialist — I believe it is all going to pan out in the end!" The important thing to remember is that we have a great hope. There are certain things that we can be sure of:

Jesus will come back visibly and physically
Acts 1:11

"Men of Galilee," they said, "why do you stand here looking into the sky? This same Jesus, who has been taken from you into heaven, will come back in the same way you have seen him go into heaven." NIV

Satan and the powers of Darkness will not win
Romans 16:20

The God of peace will soon crush Satan under your feet. NIV

Revelation 20:1-2

1 And I saw an angel coming down out of heaven, having the key to the Abyss and holding in his hand a great chain. 2 He seized the dragon, that ancient serpent, who is the devil, or Satan, and bound him for a thousand years. NIV

We should use the second coming of Jesus as a motivator to grow spiritually 1 John 3:2-3

2 Dear friends, now we are children of God, and what we will be has not yet been made known. But we know that when Christ appears, we shall be like him, for we shall see him as he is. 3 All who have this hope in him purify themselves, just as he is pure. NIV

We should use the second coming of Jesus to comfort us at the loss of our loved ones

1 Thessalonians 4:13-18

13 Brothers and sisters, we do not want you to be uninformed about those who sleep in death, so that you do not grieve like the rest of mankind, who have no hope. 14 For we believe that Jesus died and rose again, and so

we believe that God will bring with Jesus those who have fallen asleep in him. 15 According to the Lord's word, we tell you that we who are still alive, who are left until the coming of the Lord, will certainly not precede those who have fallen asleep. 16 For the Lord himself will come down from heaven, with a loud command, with the voice of the archangel and with the trumpet call of God, and the dead in Christ will rise first. 17 After that, we who are still alive and are left will be caught up together with them in the clouds to meet the Lord in the air. And so we will be with the Lord forever. 18 Therefore encourage one another with these words. NIV

In my life I have experienced many wonderful moments. There have been times of great excitement and joy; I have seen my children born and watched those children have children of their own. I have friends that have loved me and supported me in my life. When I look over my shoulder, I see so many wonderful scenes that have occurred during my life. I see my future wife walking down the aisle at my wedding. I see scores of people standing in front of me as I preached and taught God's word. I see my sons playing basketball or football in the yard. My life has been rich and full. My life reminds me of the song that was performed by the Pat Terry group in the late 70s entitled "Happy Man." This powerful song was also performed by legendary vocalist B.J. Thomas. The song is about a man that reflects on his life at the death of his spouse.

Happy Man— *B.J. Thomas*

When I die there won't be much
To salvage from my earnings
I never had a lot of land or houses to my name
I've never been a corporate prince
On Madison and New York
I never held a diamond in my hand

But I've seen children laughing
As only children can
And I've known my Creator
And I've been a happy man

I never really loved the way I saw it in the movies
But I had myself a woman of my own
The place we lived was modest
And we kept the yard together
I never traveled far from my hometown

But I've heard music playing
That made me understand
And touched the hearts of heaven
And I've been a happy man

Life has had it's hard times
When I've felt the chill of winter
I can't forget the night
When my sweet Julie slipped away

I love this song because it celebrates the beauty of life. I loved it when I was young, and I love it now. It summarizes my life in so many ways. The song says that life is filled with the bitter and the sweet. The song writer says, "life has had its hard times

When I've felt the chill of winter." I have experienced pain and disappointment in my life, but I've also experienced exuberant moments; I think everyone does. I am an optimist and I believe that my life has so many positive things yet to occur. You and I can have hope because God is a God of hope.

He has His eye on the sparrow and He has His eye on you! He has great plans for us in the midst of our suffering and pain. He has a plan even when we cannot see it. He had a plan when Jesus was put in the tomb on that dark Friday. No one could see His plan, but God had a plan; He always does. God's plan was greater than anyone ever could imagine.

He raised Jesus from the dead and His excited disciples spread the good news across the Roman empire. God took the worst moment in history and used it for our salvation and deliverance. God is a God of Hope so you can be a person of hope.

Discussion Questions

1. Explain what the cyclical view of history is in comparison to the linear view of history.
2. What aspects of the second coming of Jesus can we be certain of?
3. What type of things will Jesus change when he is ruling this planet?
4. Life is a mixture of the good and bad. When you look over your shoulder to the past, what great moments come to mind?
5. Why does the resurrection of Jesus signal that we can perpetually be people of hope?

Epilogue / Revised

Living without hope is the most painful and devastating condition that anyone can ever experience. I have been there a few times, as I know you have as well. When we lose hope in dealing with painful relationships, overcoming a stubborn habit or sins, or we just view life as heading toward a brick wall, we can feel depressed and overwhelmed. When we are surrounded by constant bad news, as with the COVID pandemic that began in 2020, we can feel that we are living life under a dark cloud that seems to get darker and darker by the hour. People that feel hopeless have the sense of being in a dark room with no windows and doors; they feel that there is no way out.

I remember a wonderful sixteen-year-old girl in our church when I was a very young pastor; her name was Kim. Her family received devastating news one day that she had a large, cancerous tumor in her abdomen the size of a volleyball, and that her condition was terminal. After this morbid diagnosis, Kim was taken to John Hopkins University Hospital in Baltimore, Maryland. Immediately after she was admitted, her condition worsened and Kim had emergency surgery to remove the tumor. Her parents were frantic and looked to me to offer some solace.

This was my first traumatic situation as a young pastor. All I could offer them was that I would mobilize our small church to pray. Karen and I, as well as dozens of people from the church, made the two-hour drive to the hospital to hold a prayer vigil.

There was no nearby chapel for us to pray in, so we used the hospital waiting room for our prayer meeting.

I distinctly remember the wonderful people of our church that prayed throughout the entire night for Kim's recovery. There were dozens of people spread in various positions praying for this young girl. As we prayed, I was reminded of the passage in the book of Acts when Peter was in jail awaiting probable execution by Herod Antipas (Acts 12:6-19). The passage says that while Peter was in jail, the church prayed earnestly for him. The church was no doubt motivated to pray because Herod had just killed James, another dynamic apostle of the early church (Acts 12:1-5). As the church prayed, the Lord moved on Peter's behalf. Then, in the middle of the night, an angel came to Peter and caused the chains, which were attached to the soldiers guarding him, to fall from his wrist. Peter was then led through a series of gates that miraculously opened for him. When Peter got to the street, he realized an angel had released him from a predicament that would have certainly led to his death. Peter was freed from his hopeless situation.

Peter went to the house of Mary, the mother of John Mark, where fellow Christians had been diligently praying for him. Ironically, when Peter knocked on the door and announced that he was free from prison, they failed to comprehend and believe that he was liberated from his hopeless situation. They said through the closed door, "It can't be Peter because he is still in jail." But it *was* Peter and he was free; he was liberated from the hopeless situation that he had been in. God had intervened through His mercy in answer to the prayers of the early Christians. This was the passage that came to me as I sat uncomfortably praying in the waiting room chair at John's Hopkin's University Hospital in the middle of the night. I reminded our faithful group about Peter's miraculous release from prison and that we should apply that story to Kim's situation as we prayed.

When I came back to our church on Sunday morning to preach, I told the congregation about the story of Peter in Acts 12, and we prayed that Kim would be released from her hopeless situation just as Peter had been released from his imprisonment. Amazingly that week as we prayed for Kim, she began to improve, overcoming leukemia, kidney failure, pneumonia, and paralysis. The surgeons had told our little prayer band that they had done all they could do after they performed surgery, but God continued to work in Kim's body. Three years later, Kim stood in front of me with her fiancé, Tim, and I performed their wedding.

Kim and Tim went on to have a happy marriage and increased their family by adopting four beautiful children. One of their children was a little girl they adopted from China who had been abandoned in freezing temperatures at an open-air bus stop. Thankfully, a policeman found this poor, shivering infant. Kim and Tim eventually adopted her, giving her a home filled with love. They named their little adopted Chinese daughter, Hope.

After Kim's ordeal at the hospital, she told me of a recurring dream she had when she was in a medically induced coma. She said she was in a dark room tied to a bed in the center of the room. In the dream she would attempt to untie herself. She would eventually get the ropes free from her wrists, get up out of the bed, and walk toward a door on the other side of the room. However, as soon as she would get to the door, a mysterious force would push Kim back into the bed and retie her. This happened numerous times but then something changed. The last time she got to the door, she was able to open it in her dream; she then awoke from her coma.

I couldn't help but see the similarities between Kim's dream and the story of Peter in jail from the book of Acts. Our church was in the waiting room praying for Kim as she was struggling to get out of the dark prison of her coma. The wonderful surgeons of John Hopkins University and the prayers of our church helped Kim beat her terminal illness. Although she had some residual effects from the cancer, Kim has lived a full and happy life since then. Kim eventually became a nurse so she could help others the way the nurses at the hospital had helped her.

I am very sensitive to the fact that this isn't everyone's story when praying for a loved one with cancer. The Lord takes some of our loved ones into His presence at the end of their struggle, but Kim's story is a wonderful picture of hope. This beautiful sixteen-year-old girl was without hope and in a hopeless situation, but God intervened and changed the trajectory of her life. Kim survived her ordeal, which gave her the opportunity to rescue another sweet soul with no future, a little Chinese girl that she would name Hope.

Like Kim's hideous dream, many things in life tie us to a bed in a dark room. It may be our bitterness toward someone that is difficult to forgive, it might be that we feel the world is so messed up that things will never improve, or it may be that we are tied in a bed of our own sinful habits. Regardless of what dark room you are in, there is hope. Every story and every chapter in this book represent various struggles throughout my Christian journey. I have struggled with feeling hopeless regarding relational conflicts as well as stubborn habits. I've wondered if I can be optimistic in such a dark world. The answer is yes! You can have hope! I live each day as a person of hope. My life, regardless of its struggles, has become better and better. In Proverbs, it says, "The path of the righteous is like the light of dawn, which shines brighter and brighter until the full day." (Proverbs 4:18).

There are some private stories about struggles in my life that are so painful that only a few people know about them. Each of these situations has caused me great pain and has led me to draw strength on the Lord. His comfort has never failed me. He has not only given me strength, but He has given me hope. I fully expect my future to be bright because I am linked and joined to the Father of light that expels the darkness from my mind and soul (James 1:17). Please allow me to pray for you that God would give you hope regardless of the situation that you are in.

Dear Heavenly Father,

I thank you for loving all of us perfectly. I know that you know everything about each of us and You constantly care for us as your children. You know when we feel overwhelmed by life and You know those things we think about that deeply disturb us. We are so grateful that we can cast all our cares upon You because You care for us. Lord we give You our broken relationships and the stubborn habits in our lives that do not honor You. We thank You in advance for your patience and love. We know that we are a work in progress, and because You began a good work in us, we know that You will fully complete what You began. We are grateful that history is under your sovereign direction and that You have a plan and purpose for all things. We trust You and we rest in Your wisdom, power, and strength. Fill us with constant hope so that those around us also might be people of hope and joy.

In Jesus name Amen.

Acknowledgments for Hope in a World without Hope

I would like to thank my wife Karen for her constant support and belief in my ministry of teaching as well as her insightful editing work on the final stage of this book. I wish to thank Jen Williams for designing the front and back cover of this book. I am also indebted to Suzanne Barger, my personal assistant, for the administrative details of producing this book. I am also profoundly grateful for Sonya Hewes' editorial work on the final copy of this book. I am finally eternally grateful for the wonderful people of Bay Shore Community Church whose constant hunger for more of Jesus and his Word inspire my studies and prayers to feed them God's rich word.